Sarah

Look forward to working with you —

All My Best

Suzanne

Secrets from a Body Broker

Secrets from a Body Broker

A Revealing, No-Nonsense Handbook for Hiring Managers, Recruiters, and Job Seekers

Suzanne L. Rey

iUniverse, Inc.
New York Lincoln Shanghai

Secrets from a Body Broker
A Revealing, No-Nonsense Handbook for Hiring Managers, Recruiters, and Job Seekers

Copyright © 2006 by Suzanne L. Rey

All rights reserved. No part of this book may be used or reproduced by any means, graphic, electronic, or mechanical, including photocopying, recording, taping or by any information storage retrieval system without the written permission of the publisher except in the case of brief quotations embodied in critical articles and reviews.

iUniverse books may be ordered through booksellers or by contacting:

iUniverse
2021 Pine Lake Road, Suite 100
Lincoln, NE 68512
www.iuniverse.com
1-800-Authors (1-800-288-4677)

Illustrations by Amir Bahadori
Copyright©1999 Artville LLC
All Rights Reserved

ISBN-13: 978-0-595-38149-4 (pbk)
ISBN-13: 978-0-595-85276-5 (cloth)
ISBN-13: 978-0-595-82517-2 (ebk)
ISBN-10: 0-595-38149-9 (pbk)
ISBN-10: 0-595-85276-9 (cloth)
ISBN-10: 0-595-82517-6 (ebk)

Printed in the United States of America

I dedicate this book to my father,
Major Ovid M. Rey, USAF, Ret
who has been my moral compass and
whose love has always been unconditional.

He never stopped believing in me,
even when I didn't believe in myself.

Contents

INTRODUCTION
➔ *Secret Number One* xvii

CHAPTER ONE
NEW HIRING MANAGERS: Education by Fire 1
➔ *Secret Number Two* 2
➔ Get Support from an Expert 3
➔ Hiring Manager versus Recruiter 4

CHAPTER TWO
VALUABLE ALLIES: Recruiter and Hiring Manager 5
➔ A Coordinator and Coach 6
➔ Verifying a Recruiter's Qualifications 7
➔ *Secret Number Three* 10

CHAPTER THREE
CHAOS MANAGEMENT: Chaotic Hiring Practices Are the
Tip of the Iceberg! 11
➔ There's More than Meets the Eye 11
➔ Before You Accept That Job Offer 13
➔ *Secret Number Four* 14

CHAPTER FOUR
THE 50/50 EQUATION: The Tools of the Trade 15
➔ Do You Have What It Takes? 16
➔ The Detective—50 Percent 17
➔ The Hiring Manager as Detective 18
➔ The Psychologist—50 Percent 19

- → Four Steps to Hiring the Right Candidate 20
- → Be Direct and Get to the Point 20
- → *Secret Number Five* 21

CHAPTER FIVE
WE ALL HAVE OUR HORROR STORIES: The Good, the Bad, and the Ugly 22
- → *Secret Number Six* 24

CHAPTER SIX
TYPES OF INTERVIEWS: And Their Real Purpose 25
- → Stress Interview 25
- → Telephone Interview 26
- → Face-to-Face Interview 26
- → Task-Oriented Interview 27
- → Computer-Aided Interview 27
- → Lunch Interview 28
- → Group or Panel Interview 28
- → Peer Group Interview 28
- → Interview Questions Fall into Several Categories 29

CHAPTER SEVEN
THE PERSONALITY TEST: Insight or Oversight? 30
- → *Secret Number Seven* 31

CHAPTER EIGHT
DIG A LITTLE DEEPER! Get an Edge on the Competition 32
- → *Secret Number Eight* 33
- → Discrimination Is Alive and Well 33
- → The Hidden Agenda 34
- → Identifying Hidden Motivations 35
- → *Secret Number Nine* 35

CHAPTER NINE
THE WHO FACTOR: "Who" Is Everything!..................................36
- → Everybody Has a Story..37
- → Give the Interview at Least One Hour........................39
- → Conscious, Subconscious, or Unconscious!..................40
- → *Secret Number Ten*..42

CHAPTER TEN
THE WHY FACTOR: Inside the Job Seeker's Mind..................43
- → *Secret Number Eleven*..44

CHAPTER ELEVEN
WHEN PREPARATION MEETS OPPORTUNITY: A Job Seeker's Toolkit 45
- → Attitude..45
- → Etiquette 46
- → Good Grooming 48

CHAPTER TWELVE
THE INTERVIEW PROCESS: A Comprehensive Overview 50
- → Face-to-Face Meeting..50
- → *Secret Number Twelve*..51
- → Interview Questions 51
- → *Secret Number Thirteen*......................................56
- → Rehearse, Rehearse, Rehearse...............................57
- → The One-Minute Rule 58
- → *Secret Number Fourteen*.....................................58
- → What to Ask the Interviewer 59
- → *Secret Number Fifteen*.......................................60
- → What If You Decide You Don't Want the Job?..............60
- → *Secret Number Sixteen*......................................61

CHAPTER THIRTEEN
YOUR JOB SEARCH: Done Right! 62
- → The Two-Foot Rule 65
- → *Secret Number Seventeen* 65

CHAPTER FOURTEEN
NEGOTIATING COMPENSATION: The Do's and Don'ts 66
- → Strategies for the Hiring Manager 66
- → Strategies for the Job Seeker 68
- → *Secret Number Eighteen* 70

CHAPTER FIFTEEN
DON'T ASK, DON'T TELL! Interviewing No-Nos 71
- → Hiring-Manager No-Nos 71
- → What is Legal and What is Not? 72
- → Questions You *Can* Ask a Job Applicant 72
- → Questions You (Legally!) *Cannot* Ask a Job Applicant 74
- → Job-Seeker No-Nos 76
- → *Secret Number Nineteen* 79

CHAPTER SIXTEEN
CONCLUSION 82
THE TRUTH: And Nothing But 82
- → *Secret Number Twenty* 83

APPENDIX A
EMPLOYMENT FORMS: For Hiring Managers and Recruiters 87
- → Job Order 89
- → Employer Profile 90
- → Reference Check 91
- → Applicant Contact Sheet 92
- → Interview Tracking Form 93

➔ Employer-Paid Fee Schedule and Terms..94

APPENDIX B
RÉSUMÉ AND EMPLOYMENT FORMS: For Job Seekers 95
➔ Chronological Résumé..97
➔ Functional Résumé..98
➔ Action Verbs for Résumés...99
➔ Weekly Job Search Goals..100
➔ Networking Activity Log 101
➔ Company/Industry Contacts..102

ABOUT THE AUTHOR..103

RECOMMENDED RESOURCES

Lore, Nicholas. 1998. *The Pathfinder: How to Choose or Change Your Career for a Lifetime of Satisfaction and Success.*
New York: Simon and Shuster.

Sher, Barbara and Barbara Smith. 1995. *I Could Do Anything if I Only Knew What it Was: How to Discover What You Really Want and How to Get It.*
New York: Dell Publishing.

Stein, Marky. 2002. *Fearless Interviewing: How to Win the Job by Communicating With Confidence.*
New York: The McGraw-Hill Companies.

Veruki, Peter. 1999. *The 250 Job Interview Questions: You'll Most Likely be Asked…and the Answers That Will Get You Hired.*
Massachusetts: Adams Media Corporation.

Wood, Orrin. 2003. *The Executive Job Search: A Comprehensive Handbook for Seasoned Professionals.*
New York: The McGraw-Hill Companies.

Introduction

Did you know that discrimination is the cornerstone of each and every hiring decision? Regardless of the many labor laws that were designed to eliminate discriminatory practices, hiring decisions are made by people, and people will discriminate, even at the most subconscious of levels. It's just human nature.

My name is Suzanne Rey, and I am a body broker. No, this is not a confession. I don't run illegal aliens over the Mexican border, and, no, I am not a pimp! I am, or should I more honestly say, I strive to be what transforms a marginally successful recruiter into a highly successful headhunter, or, my preferred title, body broker. The focus and emphasis of this book is twofold.

First it is about helping hiring managers, recruiters, and job seekers develop a better understanding and a more comprehensive and realistic approach to the recruiting process. Second and more importantly, it is about understanding the human element behind this process and how, through effective research and communication strategies, good solid hiring decisions can be made. If you are a job seeker, this handbook will help you to understand how hiring decisions are made and what really goes on in the minds of hiring managers and behind closed doors.

There are many obstacles to overcome when looking for employment; some we have control over, and some we don't. But even the things we can't control can give us insight into establishing a better strategy when faced with the daunting task of finding a new job.

I call myself a body broker, instead of the better-known title headhunter, to make a point: I want the whole person, not just the head! Recruiters and headhunters are essentially people brokers. There is no other commodity more complicated and unpredictable than the human animal. So to be successful as a hiring professional, recruiter, or job seeker, you should understand some things about human behavior.

For example, do you know the primary reason a hiring manager is inclined to hire one job applicant over another? Is it an applicant's qualifications? No. Years of experience? No. Background? No. Attitude? Not exactly. Personality? Not entirely. But you are getting warm! The answer is in chapter 8, but I will give you a clue: the answer is always the same, but the reason behind it is as unique as each and every human being on this planet.

If you have been responsible for the hiring of employees for any length of time, you have probably hired someone who didn't work out. If you are an independent recruiter, you know how expensive a mistake like this can be. For an in-house hiring manager, the price of replacing a bad hire is high because of down time and the potential loss of productivity that follows a bad hiring decision.

> ☑ *The more turnover within your company, the bigger the financial loss.*

One of the largest percentages of an employer's overhead cost is employee salaries, but surprisingly, most employers don't pay much attention to it. Although the majority of employers feel they are keenly focused on profit margins and the bottom line, they generally base potential profits on things like production costs and sales volumes, which are more tangible. This focus is dangerously narrow. They do not think about how much it *actually* costs to hire, train, and retain good employees, and how much bad hiring decisions can hurt productivity and profits over time.

During the past twenty years I have been witness to some pretty bad hiring decisions and, of course, I have made my share of them. I have also been witness to a surprising number of unprofessional and unethical recruitment practices from both hiring managers and recruiters. We live in the real world, and unfortunately bad things happen in the real world.

In this no-nonsense book, I will share some ideas and strategies that have worked for me and my clients over the years. All of these ideas and strategies are designed to establish a better and more honest and human connection between job seekers, employers/hiring managers, and recruiters.

Although segments of each chapter throughout this book may offer advice specifically for hiring managers or recruiters, if you are a job seeker, it is beneficial to read these chapters as well, even if you think they may not apply to you. The reason is the information in these pages is designed to give you insight into how hiring managers and recruiters interact and make hiring decisions. As a job seeker, you can use this new insight to help you understand what really goes on during the hiring process and gain new strategies to make your job search more effective.

And now, a little bit about me. Although I have twenty years of experience and formal training as an executive recruiter and human resource management consultant, I don't have a degree in psychology and have no formal training in human behavior. So, you may ask yourself, "Where does she get off thinking she is an expert on human behavior?" Well, it's simple really; it's called... *years and years* of personal experience. I have had the opportunity during these twenty years to observe and to speak, quite candidly, with literally thousands of employers and recruits. I have seen behavioral patterns emerge over and over, how people go through the same, often emotional, process. The common denominator here is that we are all people, and we are motivated by the same emotional responses, whether we are hiring or trying to get hired.

I hope you will benefit from this information, and I encourage you to contact me with your personal experiences and to share your stories, good and bad. I am always interested in hearing about the experiences of others who have survived the good, the bad, and the ugly of the hiring process.

> **Secret #1: Discrimination is the cornerstone of each and every hiring decision. This is because hiring decisions are personal decisions made by people, and people will discriminate, even at the most subconscious of levels.**

You must look into people as well as at them.
—Chesterfield

Chapter One

NEW HIRING MANAGERS:
Education by Fire

"By working faithfully eight hours a day, you may eventually get to be a boss and work twelve hours a day."

—Robert Frost

If you are a department manager, you no doubt put in many hours at the office. At the end of the week, you probably still have a pile of forms, memos, and correspondence a mile high on your desk, numerous issues to hash out with your staff and your boss, and dozens of e-mails you haven't had a chance to respond to. Adding to your list of to-dos, along with training, motivating, delegating, and evaluating your subordinates, you are in charge of staffing your department. You are supposed to know how to effectively recruit, screen, and hire new talent, even if you've never been in a management position before. In addition, the process of hiring someone requires research and planning and, if done right, is time-consuming at best.

Every day thousands of employees receive promotions into management positions for the first time. The majority of these new managers have little or no experience managing and motivating employees, much less handling the sensitive issues that can arise during the hiring process. Even the majority of experienced managers have never had formal training or been given established staffing guidelines. This responsibility becomes a new part of a manager's job description. New managers are expected to magically know what to do.

In addition, most companies are not proactive in their recruiting practices. Instead, companies tend to be reactive, usually functioning in panic mode, trying to fill surprise openings. News Flash! The days of the loyal twenty-year employee are gone. Most people will have at least ten different jobs in their lifetime.

Successful recruitment strategies don't get anywhere near the attention they deserve, but these strategies can save a company thousands, even millions of dollars over time. Less turnover increases productivity and that translates into higher profits. Considering the lack of forward planning in effective management training and hiring strategies, it surprises me how so many companies, struggling under the chaos, continue to do nothing to improve. I believe this is true because the majority of business owners have difficulty justifying spending money and time on something as intangible as training. In other words, unless a business expense can translate directly into bottom-line profits, such as sales revenues, it is not perceived as important. So chaotic hiring practices have become the norm, and apparently this haphazard approach isn't going to change any time soon.

Hiring managers are basically left to their own devices. Fortunately, even without the support of senior management, there are a number of things a hiring manager can do.

> **Secret #2: A large percentage of managers who are in charge of hiring have little or no formal training in the interviewing and hiring process.**

It's important for job seekers to understand this secret. Job seekers must prepare themselves as much as possible for an interview, because odds are at some point they will be interviewed by someone who is shooting from the hip. The more job applicants can control the interview, the better their chances will be for a successful outcome. I will cover these strategies for job seekers in chapter 11.

**Bad hiring decisions equal high turnover.
High turnover equals reduced productivity.
Reduced productivity equals reduced profits.**

Get Support from an Expert

Fortunately most companies of a decent size have a human resources (HR) department and endorse the use of outside recruiters for key openings. If you are a hiring manager, take advantage of any available resources, internal and external. Internally, you can seek advice from your HR department. This department should have some systems in place for conducting a search for new talent. Outside support is also essential, in the forms of using external educational training and retaining a recruitment consultant, especially if a company is looking for senior level or hard-to-find individuals.

When looking for professional talent, adding the eyes and ears of an outside consultant to your arsenal of tools has many advantages. Besides being a knowledgeable source for the hiring process, in many job markets the best potential candidates are most likely employed and are neither seeking a new position nor answering ads. An outside consultant can bring your position and its benefits to a passive candidate's attention. In addition, a consultant will take on the most time-consuming and difficult part of the recruitment process: identifying the most qualified candidates who have an interest in the position. This kind of support can save a hiring manager a great deal of time. Of course, outside consultants do come with a price or fee, but this expense is worthwhile in gaining the expertise of a knowledgeable, well-connected recruiter who is familiar with the manager's industry.

Even organizations that have in-house recruiters or staffing managers often use the support of an independent hiring consultant. The reason for this is that in-house recruiters are full-time employees and are *ethically* not supposed to contact their competitors directly to recruit job candidates. In-house recruiters typically post internal job openings, post jobs on Internet sites, conduct Internet searches, place ads in newspapers and trade publications, and attend career fairs. Many organizations also retain an independent recruiter who can do what an in-house recruiter cannot ethically do: *recruit talent from their competitors.*

Job seekers can also benefit when being represented by a recruiter. If a recruiter has a strong working relationship with the hiring manager, the recruiter can provide a job seeker with much more information about the position and can offer insight into the hiring manager's personality and background, the dynamics of the department, and the organization's corporate philosophy, as well as the qualifications, skills, and other elements the hiring manager is really looking for. I will go into more detail about this in chapter 8.

Hiring Manager versus Recruiter

The relationship between hiring managers and recruiters is often adversarial. I have heard many a manager tell me that recruiters are a necessary evil and that recruitment fees are too high. This perception is understandable because many recruiters don't have the know-how to establish themselves as a vital part of the hiring manager's team throughout the recruitment process. Often, managers who don't think they need help are the ones who have the largest turnover in their departments. They believe that turnover is part of being in business and never think it might have something to do with bad hiring decisions.

Smart hiring managers realize they can't do everything by themselves, and they are not afraid to ask for support. The trick is to find a consultant who can deliver the best service possible. A great recruiter is a personal coach and hiring consultant who can guide the manager through every step of the process.

Corporations throughout the United States are utilizing consultants more than ever, in every area and every business unit, from management consulting to sales and marketing. With the increasing cost of employee benefits, using consultants has become more attractive than hiring full-time employees because the company is able to hire the expertise it needs for only as long as needed, without paying payroll taxes and providing medical, dental, and other employee benefits. Outsourcing is the future…and the future is already here.

Chapter Two

VALUABLE ALLIES:
Recruiter and Hiring Manager

Hiring managers often don't realize what a valuable ally a good recruiter can be, primarily because managers don't know how to screen, select, and utilize a recruiter effectively. An accomplished recruiter is thorough and knowledgeable, and has excellent follow through.

> ☑ A good recruiter is a broker, the middleman who artfully keeps the lines of communication between manager and potential new hires open and amiable until an offer has been extended and a compensation package has been agreed upon. If a recruiter offers this level of expertise and personal service, the manager will have a valuable ally.

Before conducting a search, a recruiter should obtain the following information from the hiring manager:

1. Who the hiring manager is. This information includes the manager's professional and personal background, history and experience with the company, personal interests and hobbies, and other relevant details.
2. The manager's hiring needs. The recruiter should understand not only *what* the hiring manager is looking for, but also *why*. Is the

company growing? Is the organization replacing someone who left? Was someone terminated, and if so, why?
3. The company's philosophy, structure, and business objectives. What is the internal personality of the company? What is the company's primary business function? What are the company's current and future goals? What is the general management style? What are the company's subsidiaries and divisions?
4. The manager's department. How is it structured? Who are the team of people a new hire will be interacting with?
5. The company's competitors. Who is the competition, and how do they differ?

This kind of vital information gives a recruiter the knowledge to effectively conduct a search on behalf of the hiring manager as well as to offer insight to the candidates who will be interviewing for the job.

A Coordinator and Coach

A recruiter should be educated and knowledgeable enough to be a coordinator and coach for both the hiring manager and candidates throughout the selection and placement process. A hiring manager should expect the recruiter to take the following responsibilities:

- Research the client's competitors to identify at least three to five potential candidates who are qualified for and interested in the position.
- Conduct the recruitment and preliminary screening of each potential candidate.
- Schedule all interviews, and prepare both the manager and the candidate for each step in the interview process.
- Gather feedback and information about the level of interest from both the manager and the candidate after each meeting.
- Conduct formal reference checks on candidate.
- Negotiate the candidate's compensation, bonuses, perks, and benefits.
- Extend the informal offer to the candidate for feedback to prepare the manager for further negotiations, if necessary.

Verifying a Recruiter's Qualifications

If you're a hiring manager who wants to retain an outside consultant for recruitment, you should verify that the recruiter meets the following criteria:

1. Recruiter has five or more years of specialized experience recruiting within your specific industry.

2. Recruiter has a successful track record for placing candidates with the qualifications and business level of experience you are looking for (i.e., support staff level, management level, executive level, etc.). Each level requires different recruiting strategies. A recruiter who specializes in filling administrative positions may not be as successful recruiting executive candidates.

3. Recruiter has a minimum of three client references from within your industry that you can check.

4. Recruiter has an established track record for making successful placements and can demonstrate that placed candidates generally stay at their new positions for a reasonable period of time. Based on your industry practices, supply and demand, and other relevant factors, you will have to determine what a reasonable period of time is. (For my industry, a reasonable period is about two years for full-time hires, not for contractors.)

5. Recruiter should have a reasonable and competitive fee structure and guarantee. What is considered reasonable is based on supply and demand in the industry, but no recruiter should charge more than 30 percent of the annual salary of the individual hired. If a recruiter is retained with an exclusive agreement, rather than hired on a contingency basis, the hiring manager should be able to negotiate a lower fee because a retained recruiter does not have to compete with other recruiters for the same search assignment. A recruiter's *guarantee period* for a candidate should be somewhere between thirty and sixty days. (A guarantee period is the length of time a recruiter is required to replace a candidate, at no extra charge, if the candidate resigns or is terminated during that period.)

6. Recruiter should have detailed knowledge of compensation and benefits related to your industry.

7. Recruiter possesses strong negotiating skills because negotiating a candidate's compensation, perks, and benefits is a critical part of the job offer process.
8. Recruiter has excellent interpersonal and communication skills (oral and written) with those at all levels within your industry.
9. Recruiter has effective research and information-gathering skills.
10. Recruiter demonstrates consistent follow-through with both the company and candidates.
11. Recruiter has a track record for maintaining a high level of customer satisfaction.
12. Recruiter has built a good reputation in your industry and consistently demonstrates honesty, integrity, and confidentiality with both clients and candidates.

Number 12 may be last on the list, but it is the most important criterion. When you speak to those references, ask direct, specific questions about the recruiter's reputation in your industry. As you know, many laws protect employees and potential new hires, so you should make sure you are working with a recruiter who is not only knowledgeable but ethical and sensitive to the critical issues of confidentiality and to the often stressful process involved in changing jobs.

> ☑ **Changing jobs can be a very traumatic and stressful experience. It can be as stressful as moving, divorce, or the loss of a loved one; so integrity, confidentiality, and sensitivity are important qualifications to look for in recruitment professionals.**

Thousands of recruiters are available today. Each typically specializes in a specific industry (such as healthcare, information technology, manufacturing, retail, etc.). In addition, most recruiters specialize in a particular niche or level within their chosen industry; for example, in the healthcare industry, some recruit only nurses or doctors. In the information technology industry, some recruiters specialize in recruiting software developers or hardware engineers or database administrators. It's important to find a recruiter who is familiar with the manager's company and its competitors, and who has professional contacts within that particular industry.

From personal experience and from the experience of my clients and the job seekers I have represented, I have found that recruiters often fall short in three areas.

1. The recruiter does not have enough knowledge about the industry.

For a brief period I held a position as the director of career services for a college specializing in the information technology industry. My staff placed graduates in such positions as computer programmer, network administrator, and database administrator (DBA) for business applications. At first I was amazed by how many recruiters were in the information technology field. After a while, I was even more amazed to find out that many of them knew little or nothing about the technology they were recruiting for—the programming languages, operating systems, software, hardware, and other industry elements.

I remember a recruiter named Mary who called me, desperate to find a DBA (Database Administrator) for a client of hers. Needing more information, I asked, "Are you looking for a SQL, DB2, or Oracle DBA?" She said, "Yes, I think so." I asked her if she knew which it was, SQL, DB2, or Oracle. She said, "Not really. Does it matter?" "Well, Mary," I said, "only if you want to find a candidate that your client wants to hire."

If you are a recruiter, it's critical to have a detailed knowledge of the industry you specialize in. This means when given a recruiting assignment, you have a clear understanding of the job description. You should know your industry well enough to be able to visualize the daily tasks, assignments, and responsibilities the candidate will be faced with, if hired. As my conversation with Mary shows, you cannot successfully recruit technical talent, such as computer programmers, systems analysts, hardware engineers, or database administrators without an in-depth knowledge of the programming languages, systems, and equipment the candidate will be expected to know and use. Ideally, a technical recruiter should have a technical background or at the very least, a strong understanding of what different programming languages and operating systems are designed to do.

2. The recruiter does not have enough knowledge about the company being represented.

Recruiters should do their homework on the company so they can clearly understand the company's philosophy and business objectives. A recruiter who does not make this preparation may be behaving like what I call a "spaghetti slinger," someone who throws enough spaghetti against the wall that some of it is bound to stick. Such a person is driven by quantity, not quality, and is more motivated by earning money than by establishing long-term relationships. Spaghetti slingers gather a minimum amount of information and then begin to bombard the hiring manager with résumés, most of which are from unqualified, unscreened candidates. Even some in-house recruiters and staffing managers fall short of truly understanding the needs of their hiring managers and the organization's long-term goals. A hiring manager should seek a recruiter who takes the time to understand the inner workings of the company before beginning a candidate search. The hiring manager should remain available to the recruiter and should share information about the structure and personality of the organization and its specific staffing needs.

3. The recruiter does not know the personality type that is best suited for the position.

This is probably the most overlooked and the most *critical* element for a recruiter to make successful hires. I call it the Who Factor. If it is critical for a recruiter to know your company's corporate philosophy and business goals, it is even more critical for the recruiter to know *who* you are. A recruiter needs to understand your personal philosophy and your needs and desires to be successful in attracting the right candidate. For example, if you believe strongly in health and fitness, you are more likely to hire someone who is fit rather than someone who smokes or is overweight.

Understanding the Who Factor can narrow the search considerably so a recruiter can find the appropriate personality type for the position and the company. The more your recruiter knows about you and what you need (*and want*), the more effective and less time consuming the search. For more on the Who Factor, please refer to chapter 9.

> **Secret #3: Just like hiring managers, there are many recruiters who don't have the formal training and industry knowledge necessary to conduct an effective search.**

Unfortunately, inexperience and mediocrity are more common in the workplace than are experience and excellence. Whether you are a hiring manager or a job seeker, do your homework and chose a qualified recruiter who has an established reputation in your industry.

Chapter Three

CHAOS MANAGEMENT:
Chaotic Hiring Practices Are the Tip of the Iceberg!

Numerous books have been written about good management practices. With all this advice at our fingertips, mastering the art of managing and motivating others should be pretty easy, right? What I want to know is this: does anybody actually read these books? And if so, does anyone who reads these books actually apply the strategies and techniques in them? Don't get me wrong; there are some exceptional companies lucky enough to have enlightened leaders who understand people and what motivates them. But I am not talking about them; I am talking about *most* companies. Unfortunately, from my experience, companies with enlightened leadership are the exception, not the rule.

As a recruiter or a job seeker, you are going to come in contact with many managers who are either ill-prepared to hire and manage others or who have a hidden agenda, or both. Job seekers are not only faced with the uncertainty and stress of finding a job, they are also faced with the uncertainty of who they will be working for.

There's More than Meets the Eye

I have dealt directly with hundreds of hiring managers, and I never cease to be amazed by how truly clueless some of them are in dealing effectively with the people they manage. The biggest complaint from employees in the business environment is lack of communication, departmentally and company-wide. Along with recruiting and hiring issues, here are some of the inherent problems that exist in management, things many managers do that they should not do, and things managers should do, but don't.

1. The manager doesn't communicate clearly to staff what is expected of them in terms of performance and productivity.

Far too many employees are unaware of their level of performance in their jobs. Many employees I have spoken to over the years have been terminated from their jobs without knowing why.

2. The manager hires a less qualified candidate over a stronger, more qualified candidate.

Why would a manager *not* hire the most qualified candidate for the job? Often, insecure human beings don't feel comfortable hiring someone who they suspect might steal their job or outshine them in some way.

3. The manager is not qualified to handle the job of managing.

Everyone at one time or another has been subjected to the frustration of working for or with an incompetent manager. Such managers operate from a sense of insecurity, for which they usually overcompensate by pretending to know everything. The truth is the more egotistical someone is, the more insecure and often incompetent that person actually is.

4. The manager believes that the best motivation is intimidation.

I like to call this "Bully" management. The intimidating manager thinks that browbeating the staff is motivation enough for them. However, fear has never been an effective motivator. In fact, it is the biggest *non-motivator* in the workplace. An employee with a bully for a boss will usually do just enough to avoid getting into trouble. No one wins in this situation, especially the manager, because a bully manager's department is often the least productive.

5. The manager operates under the assumption that if someone wins, someone else has to lose.

This type of manager competes with the employees rather than building a cohesive team. This is also a manager that will often take credit for someone else's work.

6. Some managers are seriously lacking in ethics and integrity.

Certain managers will do whatever it takes, including lie, cheat, and take credit for the hard work of others, and will steamroll over anyone who gets in their way. They take these actions to get what they want, be it recognition, money, or power, or all three. I have been personally subjected to more than one ruthless, unethical manager during my days in the corporate world. In each case I had no choice but to quit my job, but not before I reported the manager's behavior to senior management.

7. Some managers—in fact most managers—do not think proactively nor plan ahead to anticipate future staffing needs.

Rather than planning ahead, some managers spend most of their time putting out fires, one after another, rather than actively planning the activities and goals of their department. The result is unproductive management. Managers cannot hire, manage, and motivate staff when the managers are continually taking two steps forward and one step back. This running in place takes a great deal of energy and results in little forward progress. Worst of all, it translates into lost productivity and profits.

There are, of course, many more management problems than the six I mentioned that result in bad management practices. Some problems are the micromanager, the control freak, and the manager who is always right. I could go on and on, but I think you get the point.

ON PRODUCTIVITY: NEVER MISTAKE MOTION FOR ACTION!

It is interesting to note that the Japanese business climate is one of extremely focused forward planning, short-term (1–4 years), and long-term planning (5–10 years). In the American business environment, you're lucky if there is a one-year plan in place! I have worked in a number of different corporate environments where long-term planning never seemed to be in the business plan.

Before You Accept That Job Offer

If you are a job seeker interviewing for a position, know that there is much that you need to know before you accept a job. Try to talk to or meet with as many employees as possible, especially those in the department where you will be working. Get their ideas on the company and its management style. A current employee may be reluctant to share negative information, but there are questions you can ask that should reveal enough information to help you make an educated decision about whether to accept the job or not.

Here are a few questions you might want to ask a current employee:

- What do you like best about the company?
- What is the company's corporate goal or mission?
- Does your company promote from within?
- What would you change about your job, if you could?
- Tell me about your manager. What is he/she like?
- What is his/her management style?
- What do you like best about your department?
- What about your department would you change, if you could?
- What do you like best about your job?
- What do you like least about your job?
- Do you feel this company offers strong growth potential?

The process of finding a good job is difficult, so be sure you are making the right decision before you accept a position. Find out as much as you can about who you will be working for and who you will be working with. Remember that getting a job is one thing, but being happy with the job and keeping it is another.

Personal management styles are just that, personal. Each person's approach to managing others is based on individual personality traits and life experience.

> **Secret #4: Managers make hiring decisions based on their own personal likes, dislikes, and life experiences. Most hiring decisions in the workplace are based on these hidden, emotionally based personal agendas.**

This is why you can't take it personally if an interviewer chooses not to hire you. If you have a mustache and the interviewer does not like facial hair, there is a good chance you won't get hired. There is also a good chance you will never know why you were passed over. So, you must get over it and move on. The next person who interviews you might love facial hair!

Chapter Four

THE 50/50 EQUATION:
The Tools of the Trade

I've had insightful discussions with colleagues over the years about what makes for excellence in the workplace. What knowledge, experience, and personality traits make for a great manager? And what makes for a great leader? Many think the answer is the same for both, but I disagree. There is a huge difference between a great manager and a great leader.

I believe leaders are born because I don't think all leadership traits can be learned. Can you learn to be a visionary? I think not! You either have this quality, or more accurately this gift, or you don't. Also, some people possess the natural instinct to accurately read others' behavior and motivation, a critical component of the recruitment process. Although instinct is inherently strong in some people, developing one's instinct or intuition is something that *can* be learned, at least to a degree. I bring up these personality traits to make a point.

In my experience there are certain intrinsic traits and people skills that make a hiring manager or a recruitment professional successful, but anyone can learn the recruitment process. In addition, with a little effort, anyone in management can learn a number of smart and effective hiring strategies. But the most talented recruiters, the best of the best in the recruitment game, are 50 percent detective and 50 percent psychologist. They fit what I call the 50/50 Equation.

Take a few minutes to do an honest evaluation of your best and most developed people skills, as well as your worst. The more you can read and truly understand and communicate with others, the more natural and enjoyable the entire process of interacting with others becomes. If you are a job seeker, strong communication and people skills will serve you well during the interview process and in the workplace after you are hired.

Communication skills and people skills are very different abilities. Communication, by definition, is the ability to transmit and receive information. In the *Merriam-Webster Dictionary, Home and Office Edition,* it simply states that communication is "the exchange of information or opinions; an act of transmitting." In the recruitment field, communication is more than that. It is the ability to transmit information *effectively.*

People skills are much more. In the same dictionary, the definition of *people* is "a body of persons (as a tribe, nation, or race) united by a common culture, sense of kinship, or political organization." In many ways, good people skills are based in the same definition. Someone with good people skills is able to find a way to connect with and relate to many different types of people by finding a common link or interest between them. This skill lays the foundation for success in many aspects of life, both personal and professional.

Do You Have What It Takes?

I am sure you have heard stories about how much money independent executive recruiters can make. Many earn well into the six, even seven figures. The job, however, is not for the meek and mild, or the weak of heart. First, you must spend a good deal of time on the telephone initiating conversations with perfect strangers every day. And independent consultants generally earn their high incomes on a contingency basis only—that is, as straight commission. They have no safety net, no steady paycheck. Independent consultants earn more because recruitment fees are based on a percentage of the candidate's annual salary, usually 20 to 30 percent, but they only earn money if they make a placement. In-house recruiters are usually salaried with a small commission for each placement, but the upside is they also have benefits (medical, dental, 401K.s, etc.) and the security of a steady paycheck. If you are intimidated by the prospect of telephoning a person you don't know and working on straight commission, you might do better as a full-time employee in a more structured environment. Either way, in-house or independent, the more you hone your communication and people skills, the more success you are likely to realize.

If you enjoy interacting with people, but are not a natural people person, developing the necessary communication skills may take you a little more time, discipline, and determination. The best barometer for knowing if you have this potential—as a recruiter or as a member of any profession you choose—is that you love the process, not just the money you can earn. If you are more focused on the money, you may have some success in the short-term, but not over the long haul. If you truly like the process, you will have the work ethic and discipline to develop the skills you need to be successful.

In addition to being a detective and a psychologist, a good recruiter or hiring manager should possess intuition. Those who have developed a strong intuition (or a gut feeling) about people are the ones who make the best hiring decisions. Notice I continue to use the word *developed*. You can develop and learn to trust your intuition just like any other skill. There are many good resources available about intuition. One that I would recommend is *Practical Intuition* by Laura Day. The real trick to learning and developing new approaches is not only to read books that can help you, but also to implement what you have learned as soon as possible. Try to go beyond spending time and money attending seminars and reading books, and put what you have learned into practice.

The Detective—50 Percent

Your job as a recruiter is to identify and track down candidates. You need to spend time investigating and researching your client's competitors that have employees with the qualifications you are looking for. Where does one find such information? The best place is your local college library, which usually has a substantial amount of reference books pertaining to every industry, often with detailed statistics on each company. You can find information such as names of principals and management staff, number of employees, divisions and subsidiaries, specialties or areas of business, annual revenues, and many other useful facts.

Another great source of information is, of course, the Internet. As nearly every company maintains an Internet site, you should also spend time searching the web to find companies by utilizing search engines such as Yahoo or Google. The best approach is to search by key words that apply to your industry. For example, in the real estate development industry, I might use key words such as; builders, construction companies, architects, land development, urban development, etc. There are also numerous recruitment and career development related Web sites that may be of support to you in finding good candidates. You can find many of these sites by conducting a key-word search with words such as; jobs, recruiting, employment, interviewing, human resources, resumes, hiring, etc. Many recruiters and hiring managers have benefited a great deal by establishing working relationships with employment Web sites such as Monster.com and CareerBuilder.com.

Once you have established a list of companies to recruit from, you need to pick up the phone, put on your private investigator's hat, and do a little sleuthing. By calling each of the companies on your list, you can ask the kind of questions that may lead you to possible candidates. This process can be challenging, but it can also be a lot of fun. I have pretended to be all sorts of different people when investigating a company for names. Sometimes I even disguise my voice or use an accent. (Yes, pretending is perhaps a nice word for lying, but this is often what a detective must do to uncover names of potential candidates.) Let me say here that this is the one and only time I advocate telling a little white lie or two. Odds are you won't get very far if you call a company and say you are a headhunter trying to recruit one of their current employees.

As an example, suppose I have a recruitment assignment to fill a director of marketing position. I will first call a company on my list and ask, "Who is your director of sales and marketing?" Surprisingly, the receptionist usually gives me the name, no questions asked. The receptionist might ask who I am and why I am calling. If so, I may use a bogus name and company name, and I invent a reason for calling. I might say something like this: *"My name is Shannon Smith with Future Visions, Inc. I asked for your marketing director's name so I can send a personalized invitation to our next private showcase. Who should I send it to?"* Usually that is enough to get the name you want.

After you are established as a recruiter in an industry and people know your name, you have no choice but to work undercover, so to speak. Many people in my industry know my name, so I often have to conduct my searches confidentially or incognito. This is when it is necessary to play detective.

After you have obtained the name of the person you are seeking, wait ten or fifteen minutes before you call back and ask for that person directly.

Another detective trick is to ask the receptionist for assistance. Most people can't resist giving out information when they have been asked for help.

The Hiring Manager as Detective

As a manager, you must also spend the time to research where to find the talent you are looking for. There are several avenues you can take:

- *Recruit on the Internet.* If your search efforts are strictly in-house, learn as much as you can about the details of recruiting via the Internet. Internet recruiting is an art and can be effective, but it can also become quite expensive if you aren't sure how and where to find viable candidates. There are plenty of useful books in the library and on the Internet about online recruiting that can put you on the right track.

- *Advertise.* You must learn how to write strong, enticing recruitment ads for both print and the Internet and know where to place them for maximum exposure. Post recruitment ads not only in the local newspaper, but also in trade publications and business journals.
- *Participate in career fairs.* Recruit at professional career fairs geared toward your industry. College recruiting is an excellent alternative when you are looking for junior level or administrative level talent or if your company likes to grow its own talent. Some of my most successful clients have a formal college-recruiting program. Recruiting college graduates and developing your own talent gives you an edge because the graduate learns your way of doing business. Another positive result of college recruiting is it breeds more commitment and long-term loyalty.
- *Contract with an independent recruiter.* This gives you an advantage because you can't ethically recruit directly from your competitors, but an independent *can* contact your competitors and conduct a search on your behalf.

The best approach is usually a combination of all the above methods, depending upon the type and level of positions you are trying to fill. A general rule to keep in mind is that the more senior the position, the more likely you will have greater success working with a recruiter in addition to placing recruitment ads. The reason is that most people in executive-level positions seldom respond to ads, even if they are actively looking to make a move. Generally, people at this level are used to being represented by a recruiter, and they also have a much higher profile, so confidentiality is a greater concern, and working with a professional recruiter allows for more anonymity.

The Psychologist—50 Percent

As a recruiter or hiring manager, the psychologist in you needs to know how to determine the Who Factor. You need to determine who someone is in order to make an educated hiring decision. Is this candidate a good fit for your company in terms of business philosophy, attitude, and personality?

If so, the next step is to understand the Why Factor, which concerns motivation to make a job change. You need to ask the kind of questions that will give you a glimpse into the psyche of the candidate. Who the candidate is and why he or she is motivated to make a change will tell you if this person is a viable new hire.

I cover these topics in detail in chapter 9: "The Who Factor," and chapter 10: "The Why Factor."

Four Steps to Hiring the Right Candidate

Once you have identified two or three promising candidates who have indicated an interest in interviewing for the position, you need to determine if each candidate has the following characteristics:

1. The right professional and academic qualifications.
2. The right personality and philosophical match for the company.
3. The right motivation to make a move.
4. Current compensation that is within, or less than, what your company is willing to pay. (Information on negotiating compensation is presented in chapter 14.)

Whether you are an independent or in-house recruiter, you must clearly understand the needs and desires of the hiring manager you are working with and of the candidates you are recruiting. If you are new to the recruiting business or are a veteran looking for additional tools to improve your recruiting percentages, I believe the key is to put more emphasis on the human factor. *Who* candidates are and *why* they want to make a move will speak volumes to you. This often hidden information is the most critical component to your success in selecting the *right* candidate, not just a qualified one.

Be Direct and Get to the Point

When contacting a potential candidate for the first time, be as direct and as candid as possible. This person is likely very busy and will get annoyed with you. I might say something like, "Hello, Michael, my name is Suzanne Rey. Do you have a moment? I would like to share some information that might be of interest to you. I am a recruiter who specializes in executive-level opportunities. I am currently working on a vice president of sales and marketing position with the Los Angeles division of a national homebuilder. The company is looking for someone who has knowledge of the Los Angeles market and has been responsible for a high volume of sales per year. I don't know if you would be interested in taking a look at this opportunity, but I would be happy to share more information with you. If not, do you know of anyone who might be qualified and interested in this position?"

One thing that might surprise you is that I rarely get a negative response from people I cold call. Almost everyone is curious and wants to stay connected to the industry. Even if the contact I call does not have a personal interest in a position, the person usually expresses genuine gratitude that I shared the information. I may not have recruited the person I called, but I have made a friend whom I can call again in the future.

Always, always remember that the most important part of developing a successful recruiting practice is networking, networking, and more networking! Every contact you make brings you that much closer to the right candidate.

If Michael had expressed a personal interest in the position, my next series of questions would have determined his level of interest, his qualifications, compensation, and, of course, his motivation for wanting making a move.

> **Secret #5: A potential new hire's personality, physical demeanor, communication skills, philosophy, and motivation are more important than professional qualifications.**

No one is likely to hire a person who is not qualified, but, believe it or not, professional qualifications are almost last on the list of importance. I have seen proof of this over and over. For example: I submitted two candidates for a job opening. One was more qualified than the other, but the less qualified candidate was hired. Why? The less qualified candidate was more enthusiastic and excited about the opportunity and was a better fit in personality. In addition, the hiring manager simply felt more comfortable with that particular candidate. Hiring managers will overlook a multitude of gaps in candidates' professional experience if they feel the candidates have the desired attitude, motivation, and drive—especially if the candidates project a high level of interest and excitement about the opportunity. Everyone wants to hire a person who is enthusiastic and genuinely wants the job.

Chapter Five

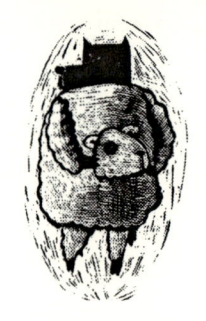

WE ALL HAVE OUR HORROR STORIES:
The Good, the Bad, and the Ugly

Even if you are an accomplished, knowledgeable, and successful hiring manager or recruiter, if you've been involved in the hiring process for any length of time, you've probably had your share of bad hires. Who hasn't?

And then there are the horror stories. Here is one of mine.

Some years ago, I managed a department for a local company. I hired someone who I thought would be a great addition to my team. In fact, I had known this person for a number of years, or so I thought. I liked her and felt comfortable with her, so I hired her without checking her references. My first mistake was that I thought I knew her well enough to forgo checking her references. I was wrong! I let my guard down because we had both worked briefly for the same company, and I knew her socially, through association meetings and an occasional lunch, but we had never worked closely or spent any length of time together.

I based my hiring decision solely on the fact that I had known her in business circles. Anyone can project a positive image from across the hall or during a short business meeting, but that image doesn't necessarily tell you anything about someone's work ethic or level of honesty or integrity, all highly critical hiring issues. What a nightmare this bad hiring decision turned out to be! I won't delve too deeply into the details, but between her demonstrations of total insubordination, inability to complete projects, improper and unprofessional conduct, and rumor-spreading about co-workers and employees, I had no choice but to put her on probation.

Instead of trying to improve, she became even more unmanageable. After she was fired, she threatened to sue and began to throw loud verbal tantrums in the lobby. It took some time for us to get her packed and out of the building, and it took weeks for the dust to settle.

My company was lucky because the threats to sue turned out to be only that, threats. Some employers, however, are *not* so lucky. Although in this situation I knew there was no legal basis for her accusations, the company was not happy about the prospect of going through arbitration or, even worse, a court battle.

My big mistake was not remaining true to the recruitment process. I got too comfortable and skipped several critical steps because I wrongly believed I knew this person. Sometimes, though, perception is a dangerous thing. What we perceive is what we believe to be true, but without hard facts and research, we are just guessing.

Bad hiring practices equal expensive mistakes in both time and money; and can be easily avoided with a better understanding of what kind of information is most important to obtain before making a hiring decision; not only in technical terms, but most of all in human terms.

As I mentioned earlier, human beings are complicated and unpredictable creatures. Many have mastered the art of projecting one specific image to the public—and an entirely different image in private. Whether as an interviewer or an interviewee, we can all be fooled by an impeccable image or a well-rehearsed response. I can't tell you that if you apply the techniques in this book, you won't be fooled or misled again. But I can tell you that you won't often be so mistaken.

During an interview, everyone attempts to put the best foot forward. Usually someone must be caught off guard before any personality flaws become apparent, and often these flaws don't appear until it is too late. So, how can you avoid making a bad hiring decision? Sometimes you can't. You can do everything right. You can ask all the right questions, be very thorough, and still end up with an employee who doesn't perform to your expectations, or worse.

> **Secret #6: It's OK to trust your gut feelings or intuition about someone, but don't let intuition take the place of doing your research and checking references before you hire, because your gut feelings just might be <u>wrong</u>.**

The key to avoiding bad hires is never to cut corners. Be thorough, and do your due diligence, even if you think you know a candidate.

Chapter Six

TYPES OF INTERVIEWS:
And Their Real Purpose

There are many interview styles, and each is designed to obtain a different type of information. Both hiring managers and job seekers should become familiar with and learn how to use these different styles effectively.

✓ Stress Interview

This is one form of interview that can give the interviewer some idea about a potential new hire's emotional state. The objective is to see how the candidate might react under pressure. A stress question could require the candidate to solve a difficult problem. The problem could be task-oriented or people-oriented. A task-oriented question might tell you whether the candidate can think quickly, on his or her feet. People-oriented questions can give you insight into how the candidate might interact with others in the workplace. Here are some examples of stress interview questions:

Task-Oriented Questions

- If you were working alone on the weekend shift and the computer network crashed, what would you do first? What would you do second? Third?
- If you had only one hour to update this old ad campaign, what would you do to update it and why?

People-Oriented Questions

- If you were short-staffed by two customer service representatives and the phone lines were backed up with customer complaints and inquiries, how would you handle the overload to ensure the customers are accommodated?
- If a co-worker in your department was gossiping and causing problems, and your manager was not aware of it, how would you handle it?
- What do you believe to be your biggest weakness?

The way someone responds to a stress question can uncover hidden personality traits, both good ones and bad ones.

Interview Secret for Job Seekers: First rule—don't panic! Understand that this is a calculated strategy to catch you off guard. Take your time answering the question. Think it through, and then answer calmly.

✓ Telephone Interview

The telephone interview is a good way to conduct preliminary screening to eliminate candidates that may not be a good match for you and your company. This approach is less time-consuming and is often used if the interviewer is looking for candidates with strong communication skills. If the candidate can't make a good impression on the telephone, probably the candidate does not have the people skills you are looking for.

Interview Secret for Job Seekers: Keep a copy of your résumé and a pad of paper next to each telephone in your house. Don't answer your telephone if you are not prepared for an on-the-spot phone interview. Let your answering machine pick up the message. This way you can gather your thoughts and prepare yourself before you return the call.

✓ Face-to-Face Interview

During the interview process, a candidate will meet one-on-one with the hiring manager and may also meet separately with several other people, including a representative from the human resources department, members of senior management, and co-workers or members of the peer group the candidate will be working with.

Interview Secret for Job Seekers: Dress professionally, and be on time. Always take several copies of your résumé and a list of references to leave with each person you meet with. Treat each interviewer with the same respect as the hiring manager. Answer questions briefly. Be prepared with questions of your own to ask each interviewer. Remember, the hiring decision goes both ways.

✓ Task-Oriented Interview

A task-oriented interview involves various types of tests that allow the candidate to demonstrate analytical or technical problem-solving skills. These tests can be administered orally, in writing or in a computer-assisted environment. Task-oriented questions can also be utilized in the stress interview.

Interview Secret for Job Seekers: Be prepared for the task-oriented interview by asking, before your scheduled interview, if any tests will be administered. In addition, depending upon the type of position you are interviewing for, prepare clean copies of previous projects or work you have completed, and take samples with you to the interview. It is important to take copies of your work so you can leave them with the interviewer.

✓ Computer-Aided Interview

Sitting at a computer, the candidate usually answers multiple-choice questions. The questions might be from an in-house computer program, or the candidate may be asked to log onto the Internet to access the questionnaire. Computer-aided interviewing is often used by organizations that hire a large volume of employees. This type of interview ensures uniformity during the initial screening process. High technology companies also use computers for technical testing and screening.

Interview Secret for Job Seekers: Based upon the type of position you are interviewing for, be prepared for computer-aided questionnaires or testing. Ask in advance how the interview will be conducted, so you will know how to prepare.

✓ Lunch Interview

The lunch interview is usually a more relaxed type of interview that gives the interviewer insight into the candidate's social skills.

Interview Secret for Job Seekers: Order a meal that is easy to eat and is not messy, so you can concentrate on listening to the interviewer. Never order alcoholic beverages, even if the interviewer does. Although this seems to be a more casual type of interview, dress professionally, be prepared, and remember why you are there.

✓ Group or Panel Interview

This type of interview can be intimidating at first and is often meant to be. Although it may not be intentional, this is also a type of stress interview. Several people will take turns asking questions.

Interview Secret for Job Seekers: Concentration is the key here. Being interviewed by one person is stressful enough, much less by a group of people. But, that is why you must stay focused. If you can, get a business card or ask for the name and title of each interviewer before the interview begins so you know who you are dealing with. Remember, you can only answer one question at a time, so relax, take a deep breath, and address each individual as they pose a question to you. Make eye contact with each person as you interact, smile, and stay calm.

✓ Peer Group Interview

This type of interview allows the candidate to interact with prospective co-workers and gather a great deal of information. This interview is designed to focus on whether these prospective co-workers think the candidate would be a good fit for the department and a good addition to the team.

Interview Secret for Job Seekers: Prepare a list of questions, such as the questions in chapter 3. This type of interview is usually arranged after you have already met the hiring manager. Take advantage of this time to learn as much as you can about the department and how each co-worker feels about the job and the company.

Interview Questions Fall into Several Categories:

- Knowledge of the position, company, and industry.
- Organizational, planning, and leadership skills.
- Problem-solving and decision-making skills.
- Communication and people skills.
- Knowledge, experience, and technical skills.

Chapter Seven

THE PERSONALITY TEST:
Insight or Oversight?

In my years as a personnel recruiter, I have reached the conclusion that the simpler, more personal the approach to the hiring process is the better. Over the last fifteen years or so, human resource professionals throughout the country have developed a myriad of formal personality evaluations for potential new hires, as well as for existing employees. A good portion of these HR formulas and tests are designed to place each candidate into one of four or five personality types. This information is supposed to give the hiring manager special insight into the personality and potential of that candidate. Let me ask you something. Do you actually believe that people can be pigeonholed into one out of only a handful of personality types?

I am not saying that some of these tests aren't effective to a degree, but I have seen formally trained or degreed human resource professionals become far too caught up in the formal HR processes of testing and evaluating people to the point of losing their own personal perspective. These HR professionals run the risk of relying too heavily on these tests by stereotyping people into a few limited categories.

On the other hand, aptitude tests and technically based tests that measure a level of knowledge or technical skill are excellent tools because they evaluate tangible abilities or skills. But even these types of tests can't reveal whether a candidate will be effective and productive on the job.

None of these tests can guarantee a good hire. Just because an interviewee scores favorably, the test hasn't necessarily identified a winner. A candidate whose test results are heavily considered during the hiring process can result in a great hire, or not. A potential hire may look good on paper, but can easily turn out to be an employee with a fatal professional disease that Denis Waitley, renowned motivational speaker, has called *permanent potential*. Waitley's term suggests that in the midst of all the processing it is easy to lose perspective on the key component of a smart hiring decision, which is the human factor.

Although I have some formal education in human resource management and do respect the education I received, I believe the HR professional uses too many formulas and processes. While I am at it, another bone I have to pick with the HR profession is the absolutely unnecessary use of HR jargon, words made up by someone to confuse us. What ever happened to the English language? Here is a good example: One HR term is *constructive discharge*. (If you ask me, this sounds more like a military term or medical diagnosis.) Translated it means an employer deliberately makes working conditions so intolerable for an employee; the employee feels forced to quit. Wouldn't it be simpler to call it what it is, a forced termination? It would be so much easier to understand for those of us who only speak English. If I had wanted to be inundated with jargon, I would have gone to law school. Human Resources should be what it says it is, *human*.

"People Hire People, Not Job Descriptions."

Understanding the human or Who Factor is much more revealing and important than a formal evaluation or test, but it does take a little more time. Nothing can take the place of making a personal connection in human terms by asking the types of questions that will tell you who the person is. The key here is not to rely too much on tests and not to jump to conclusions about someone until you have had a chance to interact on a more personal level.

> **Secret #7: Look out for the illusion of confidence. Managers are often much more confident in their own judgment than they should be. Research shows that when hiring, a manager sometimes makes snap judgments about the quality of a candidate in the first five minutes of the interview.**

Chapter Eight

DIG A LITTLE DEEPER!
Get an Edge on the Competition

Whether you are a job seeker beginning your job search, a hiring manager, or a recruiter, you must do the right kind of homework. You have to dig a little deeper to obtain the kind of information that will give you an edge over your competitors.

If you are a recruiter beginning a new recruiting assignment, how do you go about obtaining the kind of information that will give you an advantage over other recruiters? First you need to ask the right kinds of questions that will uncover hidden needs and desires. The key is to ask probing or open-ended questions about the job and the desired candidates. Here are some examples of open-ended questions:

1. <u>*What skills are most important or critical?*</u> Do you have clear list of the specific qualifications you are looking for? More importantly, do you understand which qualifications are critical to the hiring manager and which are not? Generally, a job description is a "wish list" of all the skills and qualities your client would love to have in a candidate. In a perfect world you might find the perfect candidate. In the *real* world, it is important to distinguish between what your client wishes for and what your client actually needs and will accept. Often, job requirements can be unrealistic, so you must determine which skills are critical and which are not.

> **Secret #8: Employment ads are just wish lists. Rarely does a candidate have all the qualifications listed in the ad. Usually there are only a few specific qualifications that are critical to the position. Everything else is just icing on the cake.**

2. *What qualities are most important?* What kind of professional and personal qualities should a person possess? Would someone progressive and entrepreneurial be the best fit? Would someone who can work in a very structured environment be most appropriate? These qualities determine whether someone will fit within the corporate structure and the philosophy of the organization.
3. *What kind of person does your client really want to hire?* Your hiring manager's personal preferences are important, whether or not they have anything to do with the job qualifications. From my experience, it usually doesn't. These preferences may seem less important, but if you overlook them, you've missed a lot! The information about the manager's preferences is actually about 75 percent more important than qualifications and job requirements.

Discrimination Is Alive and Well

Although there are laws that protect job applicants from discrimination, it still exists and thrives in almost every organization. When all is said and done, the hiring manager will hire the type of person he or she wants to hire, be it male or female, young or old, black, white, or yellow—no matter what the law says! It is very difficult to prove that someone was hired over someone else on the basis of discrimination. When I am gathering information from a client, I will ask off the record, "What type of person would be the ideal candidate, in your opinion?" If my client would prefer to hire a young man with a Stanford MBA, that's the type of candidate I am going to recruit.

One of my clients, whom I will call Sam, told me she really wanted to hire a young Caucasian male less than thirty years of age, preferably unmarried. She also told me that she would prefer not to hire a female. I was a bit surprised by that response. When I asked her why, she replied that she didn't think women were generally as focused as men and that she had had a woman leave because she was pregnant.

Everybody knows it's against the law to discriminate. But in the *real* world discrimination happens every day, all day long, all the time. In reality, a hiring manager can hire anyone he or she wants to hire. If Sam finds a young, unmarried Caucasian male who is a passable fit, even if he possesses only about 50 to 60 percent of the qualifications she's looking for, he has the job—even if there are other candidates who are far more qualified and would probably do a better job.

So what happened here? Sam chose to place her wants, her personal desires, and her hidden agenda ahead of her needs. Why would an educated hiring manager hire someone who is less qualified than others she has interviewed? Why would she settle for less than she had said she needed for the position?

The subconscious hidden agenda is a factor that job seekers should understand fully. No matter how well educated or how qualified you are, or how strong your communication and people skills are, if you are not a fit in the interviewer's mind, you won't get the job, period. Also, if you think you are going to get a direct answer if you ask why you were not hired, you are likely to be disappointed. If the interviewer didn't hire you because he felt you were too old, do you really think he is going to tell you? Of course not! If he did, you would have clear grounds for a lawsuit. Rarely will an interviewer tell you the real reason you were passed over. Sometimes the interviewer doesn't even know that reason. All they may know is that they felt uncomfortable with you for some reason.

The Hidden Agenda

In my introduction, I asked if you knew the primary reason why a hiring manager is more inclined to hire one job applicant over another. I asked whether that reason involved qualifications, years of experience, background, attitude, or personality. Although these criteria are certainly part of the reason, they do not constitute the final and most important reason. Simply put, the true and often subconscious reason is that the hiring manager *likes* that person more than the other candidates interviewed. This simplistic explanation may surprise you, but the decision process of hiring someone is usually based, consciously or subconsciously, at an emotional level.

Thus, a hiring manager selects the candidate with whom he or she feels most comfortable. This comfort level is often based in a subconscious sense of familiarity. If a candidate's personality, mannerisms, or physical appearance resembles other people in the hiring manager's close circle—for instance, friends and family—the manager is more likely to hire that person. But, do you think liking someone is a valid reason? No. But it's a good start, especially for a hiring manager who has developed and learned to trust instinct.

Identifying Hidden Motivations

When I am conducting a search for a client, my standard practice is to ask for a formal, written job description so I will have the specifications and professional qualifications for the position, but this information is only a small part of what I really need to know. The best way to identify the type of person a client really wants to hire is to ask for the information off the record. The key is to know *who*, not *what* the client wants to hire.

The truth is that no formal education, no book, and no workshop can overcome basic human nature, which is—in making decisions about bringing people into our lives, personally or professionally—people almost always make their choices on an *emotional* basis.

> **Secret #9: The primary and often subconscious reason a hiring manager chooses to hire one applicant over another is that he or she *likes* that person more than the other candidates interviewed.**

Chapter Nine

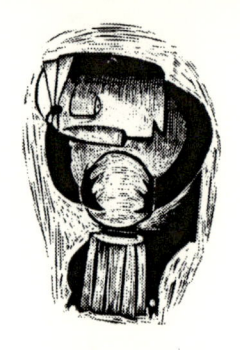

THE WHO FACTOR:
"Who" Is Everything!

If you are a hiring manager, and if most hiring decisions are based on a subconscious emotional response, how can you be sure you are making the right choice? Just because you connect with a candidate who reminds you of your beloved Aunt Sally, is she the best person for the job? Maybe...or maybe not. Obviously, you need to know much more about this person before you can reach a solid hiring decision. But the truth is that people are hired every day for this reason alone.

I have always found the differences between people fascinating. Who you are and what you are about is the most interesting information you can share with others. If you can learn who someone is, you will be able to understand that person's interests, desires, needs, and motivations. The Who Factor is everything. If you know who someone is, you will have the tools to be a more effective communicator and a better manager and co-worker.

There was a candidate I recruited for an executive position in land development. Let's call him Joe. In our initial discussion, I gave Joe a brief outline of the position so that he would be able to tell me whether he might be interested. Once his interest was established, I then proceeded to find out what really made Joe tick.

When we began discussing his motivation for finding a new opportunity, I discovered some fascinating and extremely valuable information. He explained that some months back, he had had a sky diving accident and almost lost his life. Luckily, he survived with a few broken bones. He said after that experience, he realized how short and precious life really is, and he vowed that he would not stay a day longer than necessary at his current job. Evidently, he had been unhappy for some time, and this life-changing experience gave him the confidence and motivation to look for a position where he would truly be happy. To be happy with his job was Joe's primary motivation. From that point, I knew what I needed to do for him.

I learned very early in my career as a recruiter how important the Who Factor is. One of the very first candidates I recruited for a project management position told me he was a connoisseur of classic Corvettes, having spent many years restoring them. I was very pleased to hear it because I already knew that my client, who would be interviewing him, was also a classic Corvette enthusiast. I don't think I have to tell you how the interview went. My candidate was literally hired on the spot. Of course, he also had the right qualifications for the position, but that is not what got him hired.

Everybody Has a Story

So, how do you go about obtaining such personal information about someone? It's actually quite easy. One human trait that seems to be universal is the pure enjoyment of talking about ourselves. All you need to do is to get someone going…and he or she will give you information you didn't even ask for and perhaps never wanted to know.

When I meet with a new client, my focus is first to make a friend. I focus on finding the common denominator, the interests and beliefs that make us similar and familiar to each other. In the Merriam-Webster dictionary I referenced in chapter four, it states that the definition of *familiar* is "of or relating to family" or "closely acquainted or intimate."

I will admit that finding the common denominator is not always simple. Some people I have worked with—or, more accurately, have *attempted* to work with—seem to inhabit an entirely different universe than I do.

When you find yourself face-to-face interviewing someone who seems to be completely unlike you, you must decide whether this is someone you can work with. Frankly, sometimes during the process of identifying things in common, you may find out you don't want to work with a particular candidate or client for philosophical, moral, or even ethical reasons. If you find you are uncomfortable after your first meeting with someone for any reason, my advice is move on.

To find out *who* somebody is, ask open-ended or probing questions that require a response longer than a yes or no answer. Anyone who has taken a sales training course knows how effective open-ended questions can be. Open-ended questions usually start with what, where, how, or why. Here are my twenty-five best examples of open-ended questions a hiring manager might ask a job applicant:

1. What is your professional background?
2. What do you like most about your current job?
3. What do you like the least about your current job?
4. What are you most interested in doing professionally?
5. What is your management style?
6. As a manager, how do you motivate your employees?
7. What type of management style do you best respond to?
8. What are your ambitions or aspirations?
9. What are your strengths? Weaknesses?
10. Where do you see yourself in five years? Ten years?
11. If you could create the ideal job for yourself, what would you be doing?
12. What do you know about our company?
13. What do you like about our company?
14. Why do you want to work here?
15. How would you negotiate (this) bid? sale? contract?
16. How would you handle (this) dispute? situation? problem?
17. Would you give me an example of a crisis you've had to face in the workplace? How did you resolve it?
18. How do you think others would describe you? Your family and friends? Your co-workers? Your former managers?
19. Why do you want to leave your current employer?
20. What qualities or personality traits do you admire most in others?
21. What traits are most important to you, professionally?
22. If you could do or accomplish anything in your life, what would it be?
23. What motivates you?
24. What upsets you or annoys you?
25. What are you most passionate about?

Numbers 15, 16, and 17 are examples of problem-solving questions. In a job interview, problem-solving questions can be related to management, communication, and people skills, or they can be technical problems.

A recruiter should gather information from the manager who will be interviewing potential candidates by asking open-ended questions like these:

1. What is most important to you when hiring a new employee?
2. What are you looking for in a person to fill this position?
3. If you could hire the ideal candidate, what qualifications, personally and professionally, would the candidate possess?
4. Why did *you* decide to go to work for your company?
5. What do you like most about working for your company?
6. What are your company's growth plans?
7. What could a potential employee expect about a career path within your company?
8. What is the company's mission or corporate philosophy?
9. What is your personal management style?
10. What do you think your current and past employees would say about you and your management style?
11. How do you see your department developing?
12. What would a typical work week be like in your department?
13. What was your professional background prior to coming to your company?
14. What are you most passionate about?
15. What do you enjoy doing the most?

These types of questions allow for a wide range of responses, which can give you a large amount of insight into the personality, business acumen, and philosophy of the interviewer. Also, these examples should enable you to come up with many more questions that are appropriate for your particular situation and your client's work environment. A number of these questions are also useful for a job seeker to ask a hiring manager during the first interview.

Give the Interview at Least One Hour

As a manager interviewing a potential new hire, you should plan to spend at least one hour with the candidate during the first interview. If you spend any less than one hour on this first step in the process, you are wasting your time and the interviewee's time. There is no way you can learn enough about someone to make an educated decision in less time. The only exception to the one-hour rule is that if a candidate is clearly unsuited for the job you may choose to end the interview fairly early.

If you are a job seeker and do not have at least a one-hour first interview, you can safely assume the interview probably didn't go very well. If I hear that a candidate has been rushed through the interview process, I can almost guarantee that, for some reason, the hiring manager was either turned off by the candidate or determined the candidate was not a good match for the position. Once this happens, the interviewer is usually ends the interview. As a job seeker, you may have done nothing wrong during the interview. You simply don't fit into the hiring manager's hidden or subconscious criteria. Remember, when an interview doesn't go well, or you are not called back for a second interview, don't waste your time worrying, taking the situation personally, or asking why you were not considered for the position. A hiring manager will rarely tell you the real reason. You can't control how a *perfect stranger* responds to you!

Conscious, Subconscious, or Unconscious!

- **"I couldn't hire him! He wouldn't stop smiling at me! He had this perpetual grin on his face. It was creepy!"**

Over the years I've heard some wacky reasons from managers as to why they did not hire someone. I thought I had heard them all, but I am continually amazed by the vast variety of reasons I am given. Here are a few reasons (and I use this word lightly) I think you will enjoy:

- **"His belt buckle had his initials on it."** (Obviously the hiring manager was uncomfortable with the idea of hiring a cowboy.)
- **"She was too well put together."** (Do you think this hiring manager was a little insecure about her own appearance?)
- **"Did you see his socks?"** (This comment supports the advice to dress appropriately for the job you are seeking. As I note in Secret #7, the interviewer will often make a snap judgment about a candidate in the first five minutes of the interview. That isn't much time to make a good impression, so a job seeker needs to pay close attention to personal appearance.)

- **"He drives an ugly orange pickup truck!"** (Well, I have to agree that's certainly a valid reason not to hire someone.)
- **"He was too slick."** (The candidate's appearance or behavior apparently suggested a possible lack of integrity or honesty. Even a candidate who seems to have all the right things to say can come across as disingenuous.)
- **"She was wearing red."** (The hiring manager obviously dislikes red or feels it's an inappropriate color to wear to an interview. Again, the way a job seeker appears *physically* can make or break his or her chances for success.)
- **"He was so tall!"** (Who could have guessed this hiring manager was intimidated by tall people?)
- **"She said she was a vegetarian. I can't hire someone who is not going to assert herself."** (I call this jumping to conclusions. I'm not sure, but I don't think anyone has ever proven that eating meat will make you more assertive, but obviously some people believe it.)
- **"He told me he played guitar in his spare time. I don't think he would fit in."** (Did this manager have a bad experience with a musician?)
- **"Someone that pretty can't be very bright."** (The hiring manager is either jumping to conclusions or is revealing a high level of insecurity.)
- **"She said she was willing to do whatever it takes to get the job. She obviously has no moral values."** (Either the candidate was actually soliciting, or this hiring manager didn't understand what the applicant meant.)
- **"I didn't like his demeanor. He crossed his legs like a woman."** (Could this manager be a bit homophobic?)
- **"She was too aggressive."** (This manager may be easily intimidated, or she may have had a genuine concern regarding the candidate's communication skills.)
- **"I didn't like him."** (This is what it all comes down to. There is no need to ask why.)
- **"He reminds me of my ex-husband."** (This was an obviously emotional response and, for this manager, a deal breaker.)

As you can see, these were all emotional responses from hiring managers, who apparently made assumptions based on their own subconscious agendas. Responses like these would be amusing, if they weren't so frustrating. Over the years, I have seen managers reject some of the most qualified, professional, and competent candidates. What this tells us is that the best credentials can't compete with a manager's subconscious desires. There is no way of knowing whether hiring manager and job candidate can establish the desired level of comfort during the interview.

> As Forrest Gump's mother might have said, "People are like a box of chocolates. You never know what you're gonna get."

Secret #10: During the first interview, focus on developing rapport and making a friend. You can do this by finding common ground, the interests and beliefs that make us similar, familiar, and comfortable with each other.

Chapter Ten

THE WHY FACTOR:
Inside the Job Seeker's Mind

The Why Factor concerns motivation. Why does someone resign from one job to accept another? You would think the primary reason is money. If so, you would be wrong. Actually, money is usually at or near the bottom of the list.

Understanding the motivation behind a candidate's job search is the key to a successful placement or new hire. Eight primary reasons motivate people to look for another job:

1. **The People.** This item is at the top of the list because *who* you work for and *who* you work with are the most critical factors in making a job change. If you find a job seeker who is unhappy with a boss or co-workers, you will find someone who is highly motivated to make a move.

2. **Work Environment.** Every work environment is different, ranging from the 8:00 to 5:00 corporate Ivy League, suit and tie, investment banking environment to the casual, good old boy, jeans and T-shirt environment, and including everything in-between. If a job seeker is working in an office environment, but prefers working in the field, you will have a motivated candidate if you have a job opening that is field-related.

3. **Corporate Philosophy.** This is the sum of the organization's ideas, mission, and convictions, code of conduct and ethics that translates directly into the way the company treats its customers and employees.

4. **The Job.** You no doubt have heard the saying, "It's not the destination; it's the journey." If an employee is unhappy or frustrated with daily job responsibilities or tasks, you'll find someone who

would probably jump at the chance to make a move. I have easily recruited thousands of candidates over the years with the promise of a more interesting and fulfilling workday.

5. **Recognition and Acknowledgement.** I cannot emphasize strongly enough that recognition and acknowledgement are such powerful retention and motivational tools, yet many managers don't understand their value and significance. People thrive on the reward of recognition for their accomplishments. A pat on the back for a job well done is a critical part of managing and retaining satisfied employees. An employee who receives little or no recognition for well-done work may be ready to seek another job.

6. **Growth Opportunities.** The best potential employees are those who are ambitious and continuously want to keep learning and growing, professionally and personally. Offering a strategic career path for new hires that allows for growth opportunities is a very strong motivator for most job seekers.

7. **Quality of Life.** This element is quite personal and can be different for everyone, so it is important to understand what quality of life means to each person. Some quality of life issues might include a flexible work schedule for a single parent, cutting commuting time by finding a job closer to home, or not having to work on weekends. Understanding a candidate's quality of life concerns can uncover strong motivations for wanting to make a job change.

8. **Compensation (and Benefits).** Notice that the money part is dead last on my list. I am not saying that money is not important; it isn't enough of a motivator all by itself. So far, I have yet to come across anyone who would make a move just for more money, the only exception being the unemployed. A person who is desperate enough will take a job they are not crazy about for a paycheck, but they will move on quickly for an opportunity that offers job satisfaction.

> **Secret #11: Money is rarely the primary motivation for changing jobs. In fact, it is often last on the list!**

Chapter Eleven

WHEN PREPARATION MEETS OPPORTUNITY:
A Job Seeker's Toolkit

How is it that some people always seem to be ahead of the rest of us? They have the perfect marriage, the perfect house, or the perfect job? Is it because they are smarter or luckier, or because they have some kind of inside information? No. It usually comes down to attitude, the first of three essential items in a job seeker's toolkit.

ATTITUDE

Your attitude can dramatically hinder or help you in your job search, as well as in your life! Attitude dictates how you approach life and its challenges. If you don't believe there are many good jobs available, guess what? You won't find them. If you don't believe you have what is needed to get that job you have always wanted, you will never get it. In other words, if you don't believe in yourself, a potential employer won't believe in you, either. Whatever you perceive can become reality. Your dreams will not come true unless you find a way to change your attitude.

A good way to move toward having a positive attitude is to set goals and keep your attention on them. Keep busy and focus on the task at hand, which is to secure not just a job, but a great job!

If you keep your calendar full and follow some of the steps described in this chapter, you will be less likely to find yourself making excuses, blaming others or the economy, or getting angry and frustrated. If your attitude falters, you can confide in someone who cares about you, such as a family member or a friend, so you can get back on track with a positive attitude. If you are serious about getting what you want, you need to understand that finding a job is a full-time job. If you follow through and do all you could be doing, you will be too busy to think about failure. Many psychologists agree that people move in the direction of what they think about the most. So, if your thoughts are negative more often than positive, you will subconsciously be driven primarily by your negative thoughts. But if your thoughts are mostly positive, you'll move in positive directions.

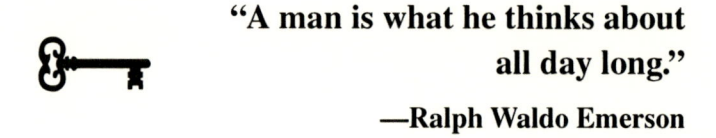

> "A man is what he thinks about all day long."
> —Ralph Waldo Emerson

Take a look at your job search strategies. Are you doing everything you could be doing? Are you proactive, or are you sending out a few résumés a week and waiting for the phone to ring? If so, you may be unemployed or working in a job you hate longer than you think. A comprehensive job search is a successful job search. There are numerous steps you can take to multiply your chances to get your name and face in front of potential employers. I will outline these strategies in chapter 13.

ETIQUETTE

Business etiquette is a critical part of understanding how to behave and conduct yourself during an interview and throughout your job search.

For example, the way you answer the telephone can often make or break your chances for a face-to-face interview. Many employers use the telephone to screen applicants, so make it a habit always to answer the phone in a pleasant, professional manner. A simple "Hello" is best. Treat a phone conversation just as you would a face-to-face interview.

If you don't have an answering machine, get one! You can't conduct a job search without one. An employer is not going to keep trying to reach you, but instead will move on to the next applicant.

When you are in a face-to-face interview, your business etiquette or code of conduct will be scrutinized very closely. The better your communication and people skills are, the better your chances for success. Here are a few pointers on business etiquette and communication skills:

- Always be polite and courteous to everyone you meet.

- Never speak negatively or criticize a past employer or a colleague.
- When meeting someone for the first time, stand up (if you are sitting down), use a firm handshake, and smile and make eye contact.
- Always try to address everyone by name, including the receptionist.
- Speak in a professional manner, and always use correct grammar. It is not appropriate to use slang of any kind. For example, answer with a proper yes or no, not yeah or nope.
- Never interrupt. Instead of thinking about what you are going to say next, listen carefully to what the interviewer is asking or saying to you.
- Listen! The secret to truly understanding an interviewer's needs and desires is to pay attention not only to what the interview says, but the ways the interviewer says it.
- Keep your appointments, and never be late. It is best to arrive about half an hour before your scheduled interview because most employers will require you to fill out a job application. Also, arriving late for anything be it professional or personal, is considered rude! Your tardiness communicates to those who are waiting for you that you have little or no concern or respect for them.
- After your interview, always follow up with a thank-you letter. You can use the thank-you letter to remind the interviewer of your qualifications and to reiterate you interest in the position. In addition, only about 20 percent of job seekers remember to send a thank-you letter at all, so stand out from that majority and remember to send yours. It will make a positive impression on the interviewer.
- Always do what you say you are going to do. If you tell someone you are going to take an action, take it! No excuses!

> **"The greatest discovery is that human beings can alter their lives by altering their attitudes of mind."**
>
> —Albert Schweitzer

Hiring managers also look for a professional, polished physical appearance. The way you present yourself in person is critical. As I have said, a manager can make snap judgments about the quality of a candidate in the first five minutes of the interview. Even if you are applying for a job that requires only casual attire, always dress professionally and groom yourself carefully.

GOOD GROOMING

Your physical appearance and demeanor can make or break you chances for success. Here are a few tips:

For Men and Women:

- Make sure you are fresh and clean from head to toe. Your hair should be clean, combed, and styled. Long hair should be pulled back and out of your face.
- Your clothes should be freshly washed or dry cleaned, including your socks and undergarments.
- Make sure your shoes are clean and polished.
- Your fingernails should be clean and trimmed.

For Women:

- Avoid long, bright-colored fingernails. Keep nails short with a light-colored or sheer nail polish.
- Your make-up should be light. Stay away from red or lipsticks that are too dark.
- Perfume should be applied lightly, if at all. Your perfume should not enter the room before you do. Keep in mind that some people are allergic to the ingredients in perfume.
- Your attire should be a dark suit (blue, brown, or black) with a light-colored blouse or shirt. A suit can be a jacket and skirt or a jacket and pants.
- Your shoes should be clean and conservative and should coordinate with the color of your suit. Do not wear open-toed shoes, shoes with chunky heels, brightly colored shoes, or trendy styles. Choose a low-heeled, solid color, closed-toe shoe.
- Always wear pantyhose in a nude or tan color.
- Less jewelry is better. Avoid large earrings, bracelets, and necklaces.

- Your handbag or purse should also be conservative. It is best to carry a small handbag and an appointment book or a briefcase, but avoid carrying large bags or too many bags.

For Men:

- Wear a dark-colored business suit with a white shirt and a conservative tie.
- Shoes should also be conservative and coordinate with the color of the business suit.
- Make sure your socks are clean and that they closely match your slacks.
- Wear cologne or aftershave sparingly, if at all.

I have titled this chapter "When Preparation Meets Opportunity" because if you don't prepare yourself for a face-to-face interview, you will miss many good opportunities. In the end, the harsh reality is that your attitude, etiquette, and grooming can make a genuine difference in your employment prospects.

Chapter Twelve

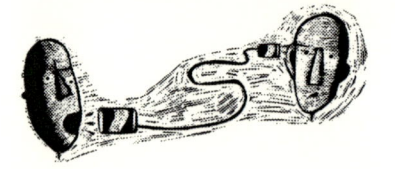

THE INTERVIEW PROCESS:
A Comprehensive Overview

Preparing for a job interview involves a number of steps. First, you must do your homework on the company. The company already has your résumé, and it is just as important for you to have the company's résumé. You can research information on a company in a number of ways:

- *The Internet.* Most organizations have an Internet Web site, which is a tremendous source for company information. An Internet site can cover everything from an organization's business profile and objectives, annual report, and revenues to the company's location, divisions and subsidiaries, in-depth profiles on key executives, and more. The Internet can also provide news, press releases, and editorials about the company and its key executives.

- *The Library.* Your local college library is one of the best sources of company information. College libraries are open to the public and may have more reference books and materials on local businesses than your city library. Use these materials by going to the reference or information desk and asking where you can find information on the company you are researching.

- *The Company.* You can go directly to the company and pick up a company brochure, marketing materials, or an annual report.

FACE-TO-FACE MEETING

Think of your first face-to-face interview as you would a blind date, for in both situations, you must create rapport with a stranger. Easier said than done! You are dealing with so many variables that even if you've done everything possible to prepare yourself, succeeding is still a challenge. Understanding this should make it easier to be cheerful about interviews that didn't go so well. Some people don't connect and are probably not meant to. I like to think that we choose people to be in our lives, personally or professionally, because of compatibility or a connection. Unfortunately, in the real world we are sometimes forced to work with people we don't like or have no connection to.

When I teach workshops on interviewing strategies, I compare a job interview to a sales call. Your job is to sell yourself and your qualifications to the interviewer. One of life's little truisms is that confidence is a magnet that attracts people. The more confident you are about your value as a strong candidate, the more likely your chances of making the short list.

Be careful not to confuse confidence with ego. Displaying a strong ego is not attractive and is a very bad strategy if you are serious about getting and keeping a job. As I said, the reason someone projects a strong ego often lies in the exact opposite, insecurity. Someone who is self-confident does not need to boast, act self-important, or behave in a cocky manner. Confidence is self-assurance, a positive attitude, and a conviction about one's own self worth.

> **Secret #12: Your first interview is very much like a blind date. If you are not able to establish a level of comfort and rapport with the interviewer, there won't be a second date nor a second interview!**

INTERVIEW QUESTIONS

Many books are dedicated to covering hundreds of job interview questions and how to answer them, so I am not going to give you a laundry list of questions in this chapter. I honestly don't think anyone can come up with all the possible interview questions you could be asked, so my focus here is to give you the tools you need to approach any given question with ease and confidence.

What I feel is more important than memorizing answers to possible questions is learning to identify the motivation behind a question. Here is a short list of a few of the most typical (and potentially challenging) questions and the motivation behind them. These can be dangerous questions because an inappropriate response to any one of these questions could take you out of the running for the job.

1. **Tell me about yourself.**

This is a very generic question (or request) that can easily be misinterpreted. What kind of information is the interviewer looking for?

The motivation: The interviewer wants to know about your professional background and accomplishments. This is not the time to talk about your favorite color or hobbies. Remember, you are in a job interview, so respond only with information that is relevant to the job you are interviewing for. Example answer: "I have been sales and marketing director for ABC Company for over ten years. Last year I spearheaded an ad campaign that successfully increased our customer base by 40 percent and our sales by 35 percent."

2. **Why do you want to leave your current position?**

The motivation: The interviewer wants to know if you have a credible reason for wanting to make a move. Here are some acceptable reasons:

- "There is no opportunity for growth in my current position."
- "My company is downsizing."
- "I am not challenged enough in my current position."
- "I am not utilizing all my skills in this position."
- "There is new ownership, and the company is changing direction."
- "The company is moving out of state, and I do not wish to move my family."

What you do not say is something negative:

- "I don't like my boss."
- "I need a job."
- "I don't like my job."
- "The company is unethical."
- "I'm tired of working there."
- "I'm looking for an easier job."
- "I don't want to drive that far anymore."
- "I want more money."

Answers like these can be construed as negative by a potential employer. You don't want the employer to think you have a negative attitude or that you are mean-spirited, lazy, or inflexible.

3.   **What would you consider to be the ideal job?**

The motivation: The employer wants to know if you would actually be happy if you accepted the job.

Hiring managers want to hire candidates who show a genuine interest in the position, because a happy employee truly is a productive employee. The best way to respond to this question is to focus on the key qualifications of the position you are interviewing for. If you describe a job that is considerably different from the one you are interviewing for, odds are you will talk yourself right out of the running.

4.   **Why do you want to work for this company?**

The motivation: The employer wants to know what you know and like about the company and why you are interested in working there.

If you've done your homework, you should have several valid reasons for your interest in the company and the position.

5.   **What are your strengths?**

The Motivation: The motivation to this question should be obvious. The hiring manager wants to know what you believe to be your best professional skills and qualities.

This should be an easy question if you have taken the time to assess your qualifications, but be careful not to sound cocky when responding. Here are a few examples of good answers:

- "One of my strongest assets is my ability to communicate at all levels in a corporate environment."
- "I have always had a do-whatever-it-takes attitude."
- "I am very detail-oriented, and I believe that my organizational skills would be a strong asset to your organization."

- "I have a track record for being a creative problem solver. I have worked hard to develop an ability to think ahead and anticipate problems."

6. **What are your weaknesses?**

The Motivation: Hiring managers know this is a tricky question, and many use it to put the pressure on you to see if you respond inappropriately.

It is understandable for most people to have trouble with this tough question. You must answer the question, but what are you going to say that won't be considered negative or a deal breaker?

The best approach to this question is to reply with a weakness that is considered benign, one that will not affect your performance on the job for which you are applying. A few responses might include:

- "In the past I have been a little too generous with my time. Now I am learning to say no politely so I don't over extend myself."
- "I have been told that sometimes I am a little too honest. I believe in being honest, but I've learned to temper it with diplomacy."
- "I have a reputation for being a workaholic, and unfortunately my home life has suffered for it in the past. I still bury myself at times, but I have learned to balance my life and work better."
- "I've been told I am too much of a perfectionist or that I'm overly organized. But I've learned to be more trusting of my decisions these days, and I don't second-guess myself as much anymore."
- "Sometimes I have trouble delegating. I tend to want to take responsibility for everything, but I am now learning to trust that the job will get done when I delegate to someone."

Notice that after I state a weakness, I continue by saying that I am learning how to better deal with it and improve my performance.

Although these examples are weaknesses, they won't be perceived as weaknesses by a potential employer. The most important key here is that your response comes from honesty. Don't invent a response just to have an answer because the hiring manager will know you're lying, and that's definitely a deal breaker!

7. Where do you want to be in five years?

The Motivation: This is what I call a comfort-level question. Your answer has to make the hiring manager feel warm and fuzzy inside. In other words, what the manager wants to hear is that you looking for a long-term professional commitment with the company. The safest thing to do is to say what the interviewer wants to hear. You might say something like this:

"In the next five years I would like to continue developing my career, and learning new skills that will contribute positively to your company. I also hope to continue my education and to take on more responsibility so I can work my way into a higher position."

This is not the time to tell the interviewer that in five years you would like to be retired and living on a boat in Hawaii! Also, if you are interviewing for a job as an accountant, you don't want to say that in five years you would like to be in sales and marketing. Another answer that can be dangerous is to say that you would like to have the hiring manager's job or be president of the company. Occasionally, employers find this answer amusing, but many don't because it can come across as cocky, so steer clear of this answer.

> **Always, always, always remember to confine your answers to what is <u>relevant</u> to the position you are interviewing for.**

8. Why should I hire you?

The Motivation: The interviewer wants to know what you can offer that would persuade him or her to hire you over other candidates. If you know enough about the job opening and what the hiring manager is really looking for, this question should not be difficult. When you answer this question, keep in mind that the response is an important part of your sales pitch. Why should the employer hire you? Sell your best qualifications that pertain to the job opening. One answer might be, "I am confident that with my background I can take on this challenge and hit the ground running. I learn extremely fast, and no one would be more dedicated, enthusiastic, or hardworking than I will."

9. What kind of compensation are you looking for?

The Motivation: This is a very tricky and dangerous question because you don't want to ask for too much and talk yourself out of a job, but you also don't want to state a figure that might turn out to be less than the company was willing to offer you. So, what do you do? My advice is *never* state a dollar figure. After you have stated a specific sum, the ball is no longer in your court. The reason for this is that during the first interview, you have no negotiating power because the manager has not yet decided to hire you; and you may have closed the door to further negotiations, which could have meant more money in your pocket.

> **Secret #13: Never give the interviewer a dollar amount when asked what you are looking for in compensation! And never make money an issue, especially in the first interview. If you do, you will have lost control of the negotiations.**

The strategy to take when you are asked about compensation is to respond with something like this:

"I am most interested in this opportunity. I believe this position is an excellent match for my qualifications and background. And if you feel I am potentially a good fit, I am sure we can come to a mutual agreement on compensation. I really don't want to make money an issue at this point."

In addition, you can respond to the money question with this question in return:

"What is your compensation range for the position?"

This way, you will know the salary range the hiring manager is hoping to stay within. If you are looking for considerably more compensation, you may need to move on and look for another opportunity.

The hiring manager will likely ask you how much you are currently earning. Give this information freely. If you don't, you will be screened out. Your current salary is always factored into a potential job offer. Generally, you can expect the offer to be anywhere from 5 to 20 percent more than what you are currently earning.

> ☑ <u>Reality Check!</u> If your current salary is $75,000 per year, don't expect an offer of $100,000, even if the hiring manager is willing to go that high.

REHEARSE, REHEARSE, REHEARSE

At this point, you know that you should envision your first interview as a blind date and that you must think like a salesperson to sell your qualifications during the first interview. But before the interview, you need to rehearse your responses as if you were an actor preparing for a theatrical production. The only difference is that you won't be doing any singing and dancing, and no one will applaud when you are done!

Your best strategy for preparing potential answers for a job interview is to do the following exercise.

Write a brief profile that describes your professional experience, career highlights, and include three to five of your strongest accomplishments. Here is a sample profile:

> <u>Background:</u> Over twenty years of experience as a human resource consultant in executive search, training and development, and outplacement, as well as a facilitator of seminars in career strategies for job seekers and effective hiring practices for hiring managers.
>
> <u>Accomplishments:</u> Have successfully generated over $200,000 in recruiting fees annually. Increased client base on an average of 25 percent per year. Published writer on career development and recruitment strategies in business and trade publications throughout California.

Memorize and rehearse the key points of your profile so that you can draw from your list during the interview. Don't memorize your statement word for word, for your presentation during the interview is likely to sound too automatic. Here is an example of a good response based upon the profile above:

Manager: "Would you tell me a little about yourself?"

Candidate: "Yes, I would be happy to. I have over twenty years of consulting experience in all areas of human resources including, training and development, executive search, and outplacement. I have generated over $200,000 in recruiting fees per year and have successfully increased my client base annually by about 25 percent. I have also developed and facilitated workshops that have been effective in helping managers make better hiring decisions".

After you have your career highlights and accomplishments committed to memory, and after you have rehearsed them, you will be more confident and relaxed during the interview. You can also be a much better listener because you won't be distracted trying to think of what to say about yourself.

Important note: Becoming an effective listener during the interview is critical. You need to clearly understand each question being asked of you so you can respond with an appropriate answer. When you prepare beforehand, not only will you become more confident with your answers, but also you won't be likely to ramble, as people often do when they are nervous and unsure how to respond. When you have your information well in mind and rehearsed, you can answer an interview question easily.

THE ONE-MINUTE RULE

Like the example response above, your answer should be no longer than one minute. If you write your profile and rehearse it carefully, you should be able to discuss your skills and key accomplishments in one minute or less.

> **Secret #14: Never respond to interview questions with long-winded answers. If your answer is longer than one minute, you will lose the interviewer's attention and jeopardize your chances of being hired.**

We are in the information age, living in a society that moves at a faster and faster pace every year. We are working harder, working longer hours, and being completely overloaded with information, so we don't have the luxury of wasting time. If your answers are brief and clear but still informative, not only will they be appreciated, they will make a positive impression.

WHAT TO ASK THE INTERVIEWER

Although the interviewer asks questions to determine if you are the right person for the job, you should also prepare a list of questions to ask the interviewer. You need to have enough information to determine whether or not you would be interested in accepting the position. While the interviewer is deciding whether you would be a good match, you should be doing the same.

A very good way to start off with the ball in your court is to ask questions early and throughout the interview. One question that can give you great insight into what the interviewer is really looking for goes something like this:

"Would you please tell me a bit more about this opportunity? What are the most important qualities and qualifications you are looking for?"

This is a good question to ask early in the interview because the answer will help uncover the interviewer's true needs and desires, as well as hidden agendas. Listen to the answer carefully. If the interviewer says, "I need someone who can learn quickly and is willing to work on weekends," you can bet these two qualities are very important to the interviewer. If you are interested in the job, be sure to mention those qualities when you answer questions. For example, explain that you have a track record for being a quick study and that you have no problem with working overtime or on weekends.

Every time you ask this question of a hiring manager, you will be amazed at the variety of answers you get. This is because everyone has different issues, needs, and desires that may be important only to them.

Here is an example of what I mean. I had a candidate, Brenda, who interviewed for a project management position with a client of mine. She was interviewed by three people—the vice president, the human resources manager, and the hiring manager. When Brenda asked this question, the vice president said his most important issue was to hire someone who had a bachelor's or master's degree. The human resources manager said that being a team player was her most important issue. The hiring manager really needed someone who could work independently, with minimal supervision. If Brenda had not asked the question to learn about these varying critical issues, she would not have been able to successfully address the individual needs of each interviewer.

When you interview, don't expect to have a blanket answer for every question. You must ask the right kind of questions to uncover the real motivations and needs of each interviewer. Then you will have the information you need to answer each question appropriately and effectively.

> **Secret #15: Every person who interviews you is unique, with individual needs and desires, both personal and professional. If you don't know what those needs and desires are, your odds of getting hired are greatly diminished.**

If you would like to land a job sooner than later, don't take shortcuts. Plan ahead. If you take this process seriously and do the hard work up front, you might even *enjoy* the job interview process.

WHAT IF YOU DECIDE YOU DON'T WANT THE JOB?

What if, during a job interview, you come to the conclusion that you are not interested in the job? Should you tell the interviewer the truth and politely excuse yourself? My answer is never to show a lack of interest during the interview. You will alienate the interviewer and, even worse, you will burn a bridge that you might want to cross someday.

I don't encourage lying, but the interview is a time when it's best to show your enthusiasm, even if you're not feeling very enthusiastic. If the interviewer gets the impression that you're not interested, at the very least the interviewer will recall you as the person who wasted their time.

My advice is to put your best foot forward, and show your interest and professionalism. If you do, the worst thing that could happen is the hiring manager may decide to offer you the job, which you may then decline to accept. Even if you don't accept the job, you have left a positive impression and have made a new friend in the industry.

The way you approach a face-to-face interview is critical. What you say is important, but even more important is *how* you say it. If you consistently show interest and enthusiasm, you will find many more opportunities coming your way. Wouldn't you rather have several job offers to choose from, instead of only one?

Secret #16: Always show interest and enthusiasm during the job interview, even if you decide you don't want the job. What's the worst thing that could happen? The hiring manager offers you the job and you turn it down. That's not so bad!

Chapter Thirteen

YOUR JOB SEARCH:
Done Right!

A proactive and effective job search encompasses a number of strategies:

☑ **Use Employment Agencies**: Send résumés and apply in person at employment agencies, temporary agencies, and executive search firms.

☑ **Answer Newspaper Classifieds**: Respond only to ads that are asking for qualifications that fit your background. Otherwise, you will spread yourself too thin and will spend far too much time spinning your wheels.

☑ **Apply Directly to the Employer**: Deliver your résumé in person. Find out who is in charge of hiring so you can leave a personal note with your résumé. In addition, a number of companies have a book of job postings in the lobby. If you see a position you want to apply for, put the job posting number at the top of your résumé before you hand it in. After a few days, call to make sure the hiring manager received your résumé.

☑ **Attend Industry Functions and Association Meetings**: I cannot emphasize enough how important it is to attend any and all functions that put you face to face with people in your industry. Be sure to take clean copies of your résumé, and take a supply of business cards to hand to anyone who may show an interest in your background.

☑ **Attend Career Fairs and College Job Fairs**: These events offer a tremendous opportunity to get face to face with employers.

☑ **Contact Your Alumni Association for Job Search Assistance**: Most college graduates have an alumni association, and many offer job search assistance and job leads. Stay active in your association because it is a valuable networking tool.

☑ **Apply with State and Government Employment Services**: There are thousands of jobs available in the public sector, and many of them are posted on the Internet. Simply type "Government Jobs" into a search engine to find hundreds of sites that list and describe federal, regional, and local government opportunities.

☑ **Research Trade Journals and Publications**: Every industry has its trade publications, most of which include a classified section with job listings. In addition, you can read these publications for industry news that can uncover potential job openings.

☑ **Attend Local Business Association Meetings**: Besides attending industry, trade, and association meetings, almost every city has a number of general business associations such as the Chamber of Commerce, Toastmasters International, American Business Women's Association, Le Tip International, American Management Association, and hundreds more. The Internet is an invaluable source for finding associations that might be worth looking into.

☑ **Go to Your Local College or University Research Library**: The college library is one of the best places to find extensive lists of industries, companies, associations, and general information on everything from A to Z. The reference desk attendant can refer you to the specific directories and business listings that may be helpful.

☑ **Post Your Résumé on Job Search Sites on the Internet**: Literally thousands of jobs and career-related sites on the Internet can offer helpful information. When searching the World Wide Web, determine whether the sites you are finding have job postings that are relevant to your background. If so, those might be good sites to post your résumé.

☑ **Customize Your Résumé for Each Job You Apply For**: Approach every job opening with an appropriate strategy that includes customizing your résumé to reflect the specific qualifications the job opening requests. The trick here is to use the same "language" the ad or job description uses. For example, if a classified ad from an advertising agency is seeking a director of marketing, at the very top of your résumé under the heading of "Objective," you should insert some variation of the following sentence: "To obtain a position with a premiere advertising agency as a director of marketing."

I call this making your résumé "screener proof." What do I mean by this? When you submit your résumé, it arrives along with hundreds of other résumés and is not always reviewed by the hiring manager at first. Instead, a manager will ask an assistant or someone in human resources to screen the résumés and submit only those from qualified candidates. The problem is the screener may overlook potentially good candidates because their career goal is not clearly stated or otherwise apparent on the résumé. So, by using the same language in the ad, no matter who reviews your résumé first, you can enhance the chances of your résumé being sent on to the hiring manager.

☑ **Get to Know Recruiters in Your Industry**: Recruiters can be a tremendous source of information about companies in your industry. Not only are recruiters aware of opportunities that are not being advertised, they can give you inside information about what companies are like as employers and which ones are best to work for. This is valuable information that can save you a lot of time and put you on the right track.

For various reasons, I will not represent quite a few companies in my industry. As an example, I choose not to represent any company that has continually high turnover. An ethical recruiter can steer you clear of these types of companies.

☑ **Network within Your Personal and Business Circles**: Networking is one of the most valuable tools in your job-search arsenal. Did you know that most of the best available jobs are not advertised and are found only through networking? The essential business activity of networking involves utilizing personal and professional contacts to help you become aware of opportunities that may not be advertised in traditional ways. Before advertising a position, employers will often network with friends in their business community to find qualified candidates. Word of mouth is the preferred approach. You can network with everyone you know, including friends, relatives, classmates, co-workers, and business associates. Rather than being shy, make an effort to be sociable with everyone you meet. You never know when a contact will turn into a great opportunity.

THE TWO-FOOT RULE

When I teach job search strategies workshops, I tell participants to remember the Two-Foot Rule. Tell everyone within two feet of you that you are looking for a new job opportunity.

Wherever you go or whatever you are doing, look for opportunities to ask for advice and support with your job search. Most people are more than happy to help. A universal rule about asking for help is that when you ask, most people find it very difficult to say no, probably because your request makes them feel important and needed. It is human nature to want to help someone who asks. So, take advantage of this human response, and ask for the help and support you need to be successful.

> **Secret #17: It's human nature to want to help someone who asks for help. It's just that simple.**

Many of us are uncomfortable with the idea of asking for help of any kind, because in certain ways asking makes us feel inadequate or vulnerable. All I can say is *get over it!* The more you reach out and ask for help, the more others will want to help you, and the more opportunities will come your way.

Chapter Fourteen

NEGOTIATING COMPENSATION:
The Do's and Don'ts

Strategies for the Hiring Manager

Negotiating compensation with a potential new hire can be a tricky balancing act because there is often a discrepancy between what you want to pay and what the new hire wants to earn. In order to establish a solid, long-term hire, you need to understand where potential deal breakers might be in the process. There will inevitably be concessions on both sides before you and the candidate arrive at a mutual agreement.

The key here is not to come to an agreement on compensation, but to extend an offer that will have the new hire enthusiastic and excited about joining your team. I have consulted with clients and negotiated compensation for thousands of candidates, and I have had to disagree with some of my clients over some very petty issues.

I can't tell you how many times I have had a client come to me with an offer that they knew the candidate would be disappointed with. The crazy part is that the offer was usually off by only $2,000 or $3,000! The last thing a company needs is a new hire who has reservations and is less than excited about the new job. My response to the hiring manager is always the same: give a candidate your best solid offer, even if it's a couple of thousand dollars more than you were hoping to pay. It is a small price for a happy, dedicated new employee.

When you are at the stage of making an offer and are working with a recruiter, first ask the recruiter to extend the offer informally. This approach provides you with a neutral mediator who can field concerns and questions and can negotiate an offer that the candidate is more likely to accept even before a formal offer is made. I have seen many potential new hires reject an offer before the hiring manager had a chance to negotiate a mutually beneficial agreement. In almost every case, with a little creative negotiating an agreement could have been reached

If you are hiring on your own, be sure to probe the potential new hire about the most important elements in accepting the offer. In other words, find out the candidate's deal breaker, which can be as simple as a rigid work schedule for a candidate who needs to pick up children from school at a certain time.

Remember that job candidates have diverse lives, as well as personal and professional needs and desires. If you show that you are sensitive to the needs and desires of a potential new hire and are somewhat flexible, not only will you have gained a happy new hire, but also you will have gained someone who is loyal to you and your organization.

Loyalty is not a term I hear much anymore in the workplace. Rarely do you find someone who has worked for the same company for more than four or five years. Perhaps our economic climate is to blame for so much moving around, but I believe the apparent lack of loyalty goes much deeper than that. One problem is that few companies truly keep their promises to their employees, yet foolishly they expect their employees to remain loyal. Another problem is that many employees have become cynical about management in general, largely because of companies' broken promises concerning raises, promotions, bonuses, incentives, enhanced benefits, and other work-related matters.

The time and expense of hiring a new employee is small compared to the expense of high turnover. If you are constantly replacing existing employees who leave, you are looking at wasted time and diminished profits.

The stability and profitability of any organization have a direct correlation to the way employees feel about their jobs. If you hire a candidate who is excited and ready to go to work, and if you treat that new person as you would a friend, someone whom you really care about, you will see a resurgence of loyalty in your workforce.

$ **They say it's money that makes the world go round, but it's people who make the money.**

Strategies for the Job Seeker

Negotiating your own job offer can be an intimidating experience. You don't want to talk yourself out of a job, and you don't want to accept less than you think you are worth. But, before we go any further, let me give you a lesson in reality. You will always think you are worth more than the amount you end up with.

If you are lucky enough to be working with a good recruiter, you will have a mediator who will negotiate the best offer for you. A knowledgeable, effective recruiter should be a buffer between you and the hiring manager and will serve as a counselor for you throughout the job offer process. By the time a formal offer is made, you should know exactly what kind of offer to expect.

Either way, the key to accepting a job offer you are satisfied with is reaching an agreement that is acceptable to both you and the hiring manager. The offer usually won't include everything you want, but you will know it is an offer you can live with.

In addition, you always need to look at the big picture. Where could the opportunity take you in three to five years? What skills will you learn that will increase your worth on the job and in the job market? Is the job itself satisfying? There are so many reasons that factor into why a job offer is a good one. As I've said, money is never the best reason to accept a job.

When the hiring manager makes you a job offer, always respond positively, even if it is not an amount you are ready to accept. Say that the offer sounds attractive, but you would first like to talk the offer over with your spouse or a family member. What you want to do here is buy a day or two so you can intelligently review the offer and determine whether it is acceptable or whether you would like to negotiate with the prospective employer. In addition, you may not have all the information you need to make a decision, such as an outline of company benefits and other details of a comprehensive compensation package.

If you are not working through a recruiter, don't be afraid to let the hiring manager know that you have a few questions and would like to sit down with the manager to clarify certain elements of the job offer. At this point you do have some negotiating power because the hiring manager has made the decision to hire you. You are the chosen candidate, so you now have some leverage.

As the candidate of choice, you will find there is usually some room for negotiation, but don't expect huge changes in the initial offer. If you are offered a salary of $60,000, don't expect an increase to $75,000. If there is room to offer more in the base salary, you can usually expect an increase to about $65,000. Sometimes, even if the first-offered salary is not negotiable, many other job elements may be. You might negotiate a signing bonus, a review with a potential raise in ninety days, or three weeks of vacation instead of two weeks. You would be surprised by the numerous things you can negotiate in a job offer.

Look at the entire job offer and review the details of the compensation package, which can include any combination of the following elements:

Monetary Rewards:

- Base annual salary
- Hourly salary with overtime
- Bonus programs
- Commissions
- Pay incentives
- Company automobile
- Auto allowance
- Gas card
- Cellular telephone
- Expense account
- Executive job termination benefits

Employee Benefits:

- Health Benefits
- Cafeteria plans
- 401(k) or 401(b) plans
- Profit sharing plans
- Stock options
- Vacation pay
- Sick pay
- Paid bereavement leave
- Family leave
- Maternity leave
- Child care
- Credit union membership

- Health club membership
- Employee training and development programs
- Tuition reimbursement
- Flextime
- Job-sharing programs
- Recreation programs
- Entertainment discounts

These are just to name a few. Benefits can come in many forms. I have seen benefits such as free haircuts, dry-cleaning, and car washes. So, go into the negotiation only after finding out what may be available to you as a new employee.

Personal Rewards:

- Promotion and growth opportunities
- Professional recognition
- Pleasant work environment and working conditions
- Rewarding and interesting work

Although personal rewards are not monetary, they are strong motivators that can affect the outcome of the job offer considerably.

> **Secret #18: Never attempt to negotiate a compensation package until you know that the hiring manager intends to extend a job offer to you. Until that time, you have no leverage, no bargaining power.**

Chapter Fifteen

DON'T ASK, DON'T TELL!
Interviewing No-Nos

There are numerous ways to botch an interview whether you are the interviewer or interviewee. Just the fact that so many hiring managers interview without an organized plan is enough of a problem. In addition, a surprising number of managers don't know what questions are inappropriate or illegal to ask a potential new hire. For these uninformed managers, avoiding lawsuits is a matter of luck. You have to wonder when their luck will run out.

Job seekers are getting savvier about laws that were designed to protect them, both before and after they are hired. From discrimination to harassment, there are numerous laws that make certain behaviors illegal in the workplace. In addition, certain questions absolutely cannot be asked during the interview process.

HIRING-MANAGER NO-NOS

Let's start with what's inappropriate during interviews. First of all, there are managers who take a one-sided view of the interview process. They consider only their own interests and feelings, not the candidate's. When given even the smallest amount of power, some managers start to believe that only their feelings, decisions, or opinions matter when conducting an interview.

I can recall numerous instances in which candidates were kept waiting, often for an hour or more past the time they were scheduled to be interviewed. Even worse, I've seen candidates, who were still employed by another company, make a grand effort to juggle current responsibilities in order to reach an interview on time, yet, without any apology, the hiring manager failed to arrive for the interview. Courtesy and respect go both ways, but for some reason, certain managers think the job seeker is lucky to have been considered at all. It shouldn't be surprising that these types of managers generally experience lack of loyalty from their subordinates and a high, constant turnover rate.

Another inappropriate, rude behavior by some hiring managers is fielding phone calls and being generally distracted during the interview. If the candidate has taken the time to come to the interview, the manager should give his or her full attention to the interview.

WHAT IS LEGAL AND WHAT IS NOT?

The law is no joke, and the laws pertaining to employment are equally serious. As a hiring manager, you must be careful to adhere to all pertinent employment laws.

The following is a list of the types of questions you can ask, and legally cannot ask:

QUESTIONS YOU *CAN* ASK A JOB APPLICANT

A. Work Experience and Responsibilities:

1. Describe a typical day at your current or past job.
2. What do you feel is the most important part of your job?
3. What do you enjoy most about your job?
4. What types of tasks take up most of your time?
5. What do you find most difficult or challenging about your job?
6. What experience from your last job can you apply here?

B. Education:

1. What were your major courses of study in junior college, college, and/or graduate school?
2. What studies most prepared you for the workplace?
3. What courses or professional training have you taken since college?
4. What plans, if any, do you have for continuing your education?
5. How has your education prepared you for this position?

C. Performance/Motivation:

1. What do you consider your most important work accomplishments?
2. What was your most challenging assignment?
3. What would your past supervisors say about your performance on the job?
4. What are your professional goals?
5. What is most interesting to you about this position?
6. What was your last work-related success? What made it successful?
7. What was your last work-related failure, and what did you learn from it?
8. Describe your ideal job in terms of job responsibilities.
9. Describe your ideal job in terms of work environment.
10. In what areas do you feel you need improvement?
11. In what areas do you feel you could make an immediate contribution to this company?
12. What parts of your job are you most passionate about?
13. What is your definition of success?

D. Planning and Organizational Skills:

1. How do you set priorities for your day?
2. What techniques do you use to set priorities for your day?
3. What was your last high-priority project? What made it a priority?
4. How good are you at delegating tasks?
5. Describe the process involved, from start to finish, of a project you have managed.
6. How have you handled disruptions or changes that affected the scheduling of a project?
7. Do you see yourself as more of a leader or a follower? Why?
8. Are you more comfortable developing new ideas or carrying them out?
9. How do you stay organized?

E. Decision Making:

1. What process do you follow when making a decision?

2. What factors do you take into account when making a decision?
3. Describe significant decisions you have made at work. What were the results?
4. When, in the past, have you made a decision without consulting your supervisor? What was the circumstance?
5. How much authority have you had in the past to make decisions on your own?
6. Where do you go or whom do you go to when you need assistance in making a decision?

F. Task-Oriented Questions:

1. Are you able, with or without accommodation, to perform the essential tasks for this job?
2. How would you perform these essential job tasks?
3. What accommodations would you need to effectively perform the essential job tasks?
4. If hired, would you be able to perform all of the essential tasks outlined and required for this position?

G. General or Closing Questions:

1. What else can you tell me about your background and experience that would be an asset to our organization?
2. Describe your understanding of the key responsibilities of this position.
3. What do you see as your greatest strengths? How would they apply to this position?
4. What else would you like to know about this position?
5. What impresses you most about this company and the position?
6. If you were offered this position, when could I expect a reply?

QUESTIONS YOU (LEGALLY!) *CANNOT* ASK A JOB APPLICANT

(Note: Some laws may vary from state to state, but to be safe, you should avoid these questions.)

1. You cannot ask the birth date of the applicant.

2. You cannot ask how old the applicant is.

   (Note: If it is a requirement of the job that the applicant be over 21 years of age, you may ask, "Are you over 21 years old? But not, "How old are you?")

3. You cannot ask how long the applicant has resided at the current address.

4. You cannot ask what the applicant's previous address was.

5. You cannot ask what church the applicant attends.

6. You cannot ask whether the applicant is married, divorced, separated, widowed, or single.

7. You cannot ask who lives with the applicant.

8. You cannot ask what the applicant's surname is.

9. You cannot ask whether the applicant has children or how many children the applicant has.

10. You cannot ask who will be caring for the applicant's children while the applicant is at work.

11. You cannot ask how old the applicant's children are.

12. You cannot ask how the applicant will get to work, unless owning a car is a requirement of the job.

    (Note: If it is required that the applicant drive a car during work hours, you may ask if the candidate has a driver's license, proof of insurance, and a good driving record.)

13. You cannot ask where the applicant's spouse works or resides.

14. You cannot ask whether the applicant has ever been arrested.

    (Note: If the position requires the applicant to work around large amounts of money or valuables, such as in a bank or a jewelry store, you may ask if the candidate has ever been convicted of a crime. You may not ask if the applicant has ever been arrested because an arrest in not a conviction.)

15. You cannot ask whether the applicant has ever served in the armed forces of another country.

16. You cannot ask whether the applicant can speak, read, or write in any foreign languages, unless issue of such languages is a requirement of the job.

17. You cannot ask how the applicant spends spare time, or what clubs or organizations the applicant belongs to.
18. You cannot ask whether the applicant has a disability.

    (Note: If it is a requirement that the applicant be able to lift fifty pounds, you can say, "This position requires that you must be able to lift at least fifty pounds. Are you able to do this?" You cannot ask, "Do you have any disabilities?")
19. You cannot ask whether the applicant owns or rents a place of residence.
20. You cannot ask for the name of the applicant's bank or for any information about the applicant's finances or outstanding loans.
21. You cannot ask whether the applicant has ever had wages garnished or declared bankruptcy.
22. You cannot ask whether the applicant has ever filed a worker's compensation claim.
23. You cannot ask the maiden name of a female applicant.
24. You cannot ask a female applicant what her husband does for a living, how much money he makes, or anything pertaining to his employment status.
25. You cannot ask a female applicant how her husband feels about her working.
26. You cannot ask a female applicant if she has children, plans to have children or to adopt children, or anything pertaining to her personal family situation.

JOB-SEEKER NO-NOS

The questions that a hiring manager cannot legally ask a job applicant also applies to the applicant. The applicant should avoid asking any of the above questions of the hiring manager as well. It goes both ways.

There are also many things job applicants do, often subconsciously, that can be self-defeating and can make the process of finding a job frustratingly long and tedious. In addition to the legal no-nos you need to understand what is working for you and what isn't.

If you are having trouble getting to the second interview, you need to take a look at several aspects of your job search to see where you are sabotaging yourself. By reviewing the following list of suggestions, you should be able to determine where you are falling short in your efforts.

A. Preliminary Job Search Strategies

1. *Is your job search comprehensive?*

    Are you doing all you can be doing to identify potential opportunities? Review the strategies in chapter 13, and make sure you are doing all you can to get yourself and your résumé to appropriate potential employers. The more you can get yourself in front of potential employers, the better. Therefore, make sure you attend as many job fairs and functions as you can.

2. *Make sure you send your résumé to the right person.*

    If you are responding to an ad requesting that you send your résumé to the human resources department, it's not specific enough! You should send your résumé to human resources, but you should also send your résumé to the hiring manager, the person you would actually be working for. How do you find out who this person is? If you are submitting your résumé for a sales position, call the company and ask the receptionist who is in charge of sales. Then send your résumé directly to that person. Taking this approach can double your odds of receiving a call.

3. *Are you following up with each person you have sent your résumé to?* A big mistake many job applicants make is to wait by the phone, hoping to receive a call. I cannot emphasize enough that you must be proactive in the job-search process. After you have sent your résumé, wait about one week, and then give the hiring manager a call directly. This approach is very effective because it separates you from those applicants who do wait by the phone, and it shows the hiring manager that you are interested in the company and the position and are a proactive self-starter.

4. *Have you done your homework?*

    If you have prepared yourself for the interview and have completed your homework on the company, your chances for a second interview increase considerably.

5. *Are you presenting a professional image?*

    Don't underestimate the power of presentation. Always present yourself professionally in dress, demeanor, and speech, no matter what position you are applying for.

6. *Are you customizing your résumé for each job opening you are applying for?*

   Make sure you are including key qualifications on your résumé that the classified ad or job description is asking for.

B. What Not to Do during the Interview

1. *During the interview, never say anything negative or derogatory about a former company or employer.*

   We have all had bad experiences in the workplace, but it is never a good idea to criticize anyone or any company where you were previously employed.

2. *Never, ever show up late for an interview!* Period.

3. *Never talk about money during the first interview or make money an issue.*

   Remember, you have little or no bargaining power during the first interview. As I stated before, let the hiring manager know what you are currently earning, only if asked. Then you can say that you are most interested in the opportunity and that you are confident that compensation can be agreed upon if the company decides you are the best candidate for the position.

4. *Don't lie about your past experience or education!* Again, period.

5. *Don't talk about anything that may be considered controversial.*

   In other words, don't volunteer personal information that is not necessary. For example, don't tell the hiring manager you are a member of the National Rifle Association or Greenpeace or The Young Republicans, or that you support abortion rights. Keep your personal and religious beliefs, political affiliations, and everything else of this nature to yourself.

6. *Don't present yourself as overly confident or self-important.*

   No one wants to hire someone with a big ego, which is actually based in insecurity. Do present yourself and respond to questions with confidence.

7. *Don't give pat answers to questions.*

   Sincerity is the key in an interview. Some answers appear insincere because they are contrived or too rehearsed. If your answers seem rehearsed, the interviewer will know it. If you respond to questions with sincerity, the interviewer will also know it.

8. *Don't ramble. Instead, listen!*

   As the saying goes, you have one mouth and two ears, so use them accordingly. Listen carefully to what the interviewer is saying or asking. If you do, you will be less likely to ramble or get off the subject.

9. *Never, ever, ever give up!*

   You need only one job, but it may take time and persistence before you find it, so don't get discouraged. Remember that failure precedes success. Finding a job is difficult at best. Finding the right job can take even longer, but the pay-off will always be worth it.

> **Secret #19:** As the saying goes, "You may need to kiss a lot of frogs before you find Prince Charming." You also may need to send out a lot of résumés and interview quite a bit before you find that one great job. But keep in mind that just as you need to find only one Prince Charming, you need to find only one good job.

The following are some serious (and some humorous) no-nos that have actually been documented by hiring managers during an interview:

👎 The applicant sat on the floor, crossed her legs, and proceeded to complete the job application.

👎 When the hiring manager asked the applicant what his hobbies were, he jumped up and started to sing.

👎 During the interview, the applicant took a hairbrush from her purse and began brushing her hair obsessively.

👎 A female applicant asked the hiring manager for his résumé and said she wanted to make sure he was qualified to judge her.

👎 A male applicant told the hiring manager that if he was hired, he would tattoo the company logo on his arm.

👎 While the hiring manager was on a brief phone call, the applicant took out a pornographic magazine and started looking at the pictures.

👎 After half an hour of the interview, the applicant asked the hiring manager if she was into swinging!"

👎 The applicant told the hiring manager he really didn't want the job, but he needed to have something to report to the unemployment office.

👎 During the interview, the applicant tried to convince the hiring manager to buy some cosmetics from a catalog.

👎 The applicant told the hiring manager that if he was not hired, something very bad would happen.

👎 The applicant interrupted the hiring manager and called his girlfriend on his cell phone to ask her advice on how he should answer a question.

👎 A male applicant winked and asked the hiring manager whether he could have her home phone number so he could call her for a date.

👎 The applicant said he wasn't interested in the job because he didn't want to work that hard.

👎 After the hiring manager told the applicant he didn't have the level of experience the company was looking for, the applicant began screaming obscenities.

👎 Trying to convince the hiring manager to hire her, a woman sat down, crossed her legs, and pulled up her skirt so she could show him the heart tattoo on her thigh.

👎 At the end of the interview, the applicant told the hiring manager, "I will give you $500 if you hire me."

Although the following no-nos are probably self-evident, they are always good to remember:

- Don't bite your nails.
- Don't fidget.
- Don't belch, pick your teeth, or do anything disgusting.
- Don't interrupt or be rude.
- Don't act distracted or uninterested.

- Don't answer your cell phone. Keep it turned off.
- Don't eat or chew gum.
- Don't flirt.
- Don't threaten.
- Don't bribe.
- Don't say, "I just need a job."
- Don't wear sexy clothing.
- Don't act too casual.
- Don't show anyone your tattoos.
- Don't tell jokes.
- Don't act as if you don't want the job, even if you don't!

As I mentioned earlier, a good rule of thumb when interviewing is always, no matter what the circumstance, to act as if you are extremely excited about the opportunity, even if you have decided halfway through the interview that you don't want the job. At the very least, you will have made a new contact in the industry. Further, you never know what role that hiring manager may play in your future.

Your primary goal should be to go into the interview with the sole intention of getting the hiring manager to like you enough to offer you the job. Even if you don't accept the job, there may be a future opportunity with that company that you might be interested in.

Chapter Sixteen

CONCLUSION

THE TRUTH: And Nothing But

In the first sentence of the first chapter, Discipline, in M. Scott Peck's brilliant work *The Road Less Traveled*, the author simply states, "Life is difficult." He goes on to say that this is one of the *greatest truths, because once we truly see and understand this truth, we can transcend it. (**The first of the four noble truths, which Buddha taught was that 'life is suffering'*).

Dr. Peck goes on to say:

> Most do not fully see this truth that life is difficult. Instead they moan more or less incessantly, noisily or subtly, about the enormity of their problems, their burdens, and their difficulties as if life were generally easy, as if life *should* be easy. They voice their belief, noisily or subtly, that their difficulties represent a unique kind of affliction that should not be and that has somehow been especially visited upon them, or else upon their families, their tribe, their class, their nation, their race, or even their species, and not upon others.
>
> *(The Road Less Traveled: A New Psychology of Love, Traditional Values and Spiritual Growth* by M. Scott Peck, 25th Anniversary Edition, 2002).

Coming to understand this truth was an epiphany for me. I share Dr. Peck's words with you so that perhaps you may also understand and apply this simple truth in your life.

The truth is…that the process of realizing success in any endeavor is difficult. Success requires discipline and hard work. Once you truly understand the challenge of reaching success, you can focus on your journey, with its ups and downs, and know that it's just part of life.

The truth is…that finding a great job, one that fulfills you every day and that you feel passionate about, is difficult. Finding and hiring the best person for a job is also difficult.

Another truth or secret that can go a long way in contributing to your success is that no matter what the situation or circumstance, you should always do more than is expected of you. Taking the extra step will take you one step closer toward excellence in everything you do. Take a little extra time to do it right. If you do, you will be the first one hired, the first one promoted, and the last one to be laid off.

In hard times, employers are forced to downsize. I have been through these ups and downs with clients many times. When a company is forced to lay off employees, the first to go are the mediocre employees, the ones who have contributed the least to the success of the company, the ones who do just enough to stay out of trouble.

> **Secret #20: <u>Always</u> do more than is expected of you. If you do, you will be the first one hired, the first one promoted, and the last one laid off. Take the extra time to do it right, because doing so will take you one step closer toward excellence in everything you do.**

Over the last twenty years as an observer of behavior in the workplace, I have seen that most of the difficulties or problems between people could have been prevented with a little more planning and attention to detail, as well as with more effective communication and people skills.

The California building industry has been a large part of my client base for a considerable part of my career as a recruiter. I have always enjoyed working with builders because they are usually entrepreneurial and not afraid to take risks. Many of them have built million-dollar, even billion-dollar companies from the ground up. But one of the unfortunate byproducts of some entrepreneurial companies is a lack of systems in place for hiring, managing, and motivating employees.

Failure to handle employee issues sensitively can result in serious consequences that range from creation of a disruptive workplace environment and lack of productivity to lawsuits and, in some cases, workplace violence. I have witnessed first-hand what disgruntled employees can do.

In one instance, a client of mine, who was president of the California division of a national homebuilder, told me that the company's owner was pushing him to lay off over fifty field employees two weeks before Christmas. I recommended to my client that he try to convince the owner to have a little compassion and wait until after the holidays. The owner of the company was not interested in my advice, and many employees were laid off before Christmas with no explanation or apologies. Interestingly, the week after Christmas, several construction trailers were mysteriously burned to the ground. Luckily no one was hurt or killed, but the owner was sent a very clear message.

It annoys the hell out of me when I hear Donald Trump say, "It's not personal, it's just business." Well, Donald, I've got news for you. *It is personal.* The truth is…it's *always* personal, and it should be! Those people who think it's OK to separate the way they behave at work from the way they behave at home are living a very big lie. How can anyone justify having a different set of ethics in the workplace than at home? A man is a hypocrite if he prides himself on being a good husband and family man, but treats his employees with less than the same level of respect.

Many companies throughout this country are hanging by a thread and don't know it. Though the fact may come as a surprise to you, most companies don't do background checks on new hires, and many companies don't even check references! They go blindly along, trusting that the odds will be on their side and that nothing bad will happen.

The truth is…bad things and inappropriate things happen in the workplace all the time. If a code of acceptable conduct is not enforced, people will take advantage, especially those in a position of power over others, whether it is legal or not. If bad behavior is not addressed and corrected, it's as good as endorsing that behavior. And unfortunately, finding people—to work with and to work for—who have a high level of integrity and compassion for others is not easy. I am afraid there are far too many people who think like Donald Trump. You've heard the saying, "All's fair in love and war." But many believe, "All's fair in love and war *and* in the workplace."

The workplace has changed in many ways. Over and over, I have seen companies frantically hiring people, and then a few months later the same companies start frantically laying people off. With many companies, growth comes in spurts, so I know that anticipating hiring needs isn't the easiest thing to do, but it's often completely ignored as if it's something they have no control over! Such organizations spend, or should I say, *waste* millions of dollars every year because of turnover and bad hiring practices. It isn't difficult to do little things like getting to know employees better, caring enough to find out what makes them tick, discovering what motivates them.

Throughout my years in this business, a monumental problem is lack of communication between manager and staff, between department managers, between senior management and management, and numerous others. The truth is...communication offers power. Understanding people better gives you the power to know how to deal with them more effectively. The ability to communicate is power. Communication is an art and a lifelong learning process. If you think about all the hours in your life that you will spend working, isn't it worth the extra hours required to fine-tune your communication skills if they can get you closer to what you want?

It is my sincere belief that if people, regardless of rank, approached each other in the workplace with more interest in *who* they are working with, instead of what duties they can perform, many problems would be solved before they even became problems.

These days, loyalty is not the rule; it's the exception. Yet most employers expect loyalty from their employees. But loyalty is not a quality to be expected; loyalty must be earned. The employer, the one doing the hiring, must earn the respect and loyalty of employees if the company wants loyalty returned.

When I first began writing this book a few years ago, I was writing it from sheer frustration—the frustration of watching people repeat, over and over, the same unconscious, self-defeating behavior. My goal here has been to offer a road map to understanding this behavior and how to move past it, so that better, more solid hiring decisions can be made involving both hiring managers and job seekers.

If a hiring manager is able to identify his own subconscious desires, needs, and personal agendas, he will be able to understand why he makes the kind of hiring decisions he does, and where he may be sabotaging himself. If he understands that he tends to have a prejudice against people who are overweight, or tends to underrate older job applicants, he can make a conscious decision not to screen these applicants out. He might find an incredibly talented employee whom he may have otherwise screened out early in the process.

The pitfall that the majority of job applicants make is to focus on the job they are interviewing for instead of taking the time to find out who they may be working for and with. They focus on unnecessary details rather than on what is most important to know when preparing for an interview.

Interviewing for a job is often an uncomfortable, unnerving experience because most job applicants perceive that the hiring manager or interviewer has the upper hand. This perception is often wrong. Remember that in Frank Baum's *The Wizard of Oz*, Dorothy and her friends were quite afraid of the Wizard until they discovered the little man hiding behind the big voice. It is important to understand that most hiring managers are just as uncomfortable as job applicants during a face-to-face interview. For job applicants, this knowledge should take some of the fear and mystery out of the interview process.

We all have the potential to be our own worst enemy, whether we want to admit it or not. We also have the potential to take whatever we have and make it better; if we take a look inside ourselves and discover what is working for us and what is not.

Life is far too short to keep making the same mistakes over and over, so even if only one of my secrets has struck a chord with you and you can benefit from it, I will know I have done my job.

Appendix A

EMPLOYMENT FORMS:
For Hiring Managers and Recruiters

I have utilized the following forms and contracts over the years. They have been most helpful to me in staying true to the recruitment and hiring process, and they remind me not cut corners.

When you have years of experience in a process, there is the danger of becoming lazy and thinking you don't really need all the support materials you did when you were a rookie. It is a mistake to deviate from what works because you will inevitably let some things fall through the cracks. I continue to revise and customize these forms according to my particular needs and the needs of my consulting business. I would advise you do the same. I have included the following forms:

- **Job Order.** This covers the primary information needed to conduct an effective job search, internally or through an outside recruitment consultant. The form not only includes the primary job requirements, but also identifies key qualifications and ideal experience.
- **Employer Profile.** Useful for both recruiters and HR managers, this form is a critical component of finding out essential information about the hiring manager—who he really is, how he feels about the company, his personal management style, and what motivates him, personally and professionally. It is part of the Who Factor research necessary to understand the true requirements for the position.
- **Reference Check.** The Reference Check reminds you to ask the questions that will support you in making an informed hiring

decision. Depending on your particular needs, you may wish to add questions that pertain to the position you are trying to fill.

- **Applicant Contact Sheet.** This form is good for both internal and external recruiters to use daily in keeping track of contacts and the results of each contact. Although I also input all contact information to a database, I begin with a handwritten contact list as I am making phone calls. This is a good way to quickly reference potential candidates I have called and spoken to.
- **Interview Tracking Form.** This form is useful for hiring managers, HR managers, and recruiters. The form provides a timeline, a list of candidates interviewed, and the result of each interview.
- **Employer-Paid Fee Schedule and Terms.** This has been my standard fee agreement for almost twenty years. It has been universally accepted by most every organization I have worked for as a consultant.

JOB ORDER

Date: _____ Company Name: _____

Contact: _____ Title: _____

Address: _____

Tele: _____ Fax: _____ E-mail: _____

Job Title: _____ Reports to: _____

Requirements and Responsibilities: _____

_____

_____

What do you think are the most important qualities in a candidate?

_____

_____

Most important qualifications? _____

_____

Ideal experience? _____

_____

_____

Salary Base Range: _____ Bonus (% and Structure): _____

_____ Health Benefits: _____

Other Benefits or Perks: _____

Notes: _____

_____

_____

EMPLOYER PROFILE

Name: _____ Title: _____

Company: _____ # of Years at Company: _____

Tele: _____ Fax: _____ E-mail: _____

Job Title: _____ Reports to: _____

What is the company's corporate philosophy? _____
_____
_____

What do you like best about your company? _____
_____
_____

Why would someone want to work for your company? _____
_____
_____

What is your management style? _____
_____

What are your overall responsibilities? _____
_____
_____

How is your department structured? _____
_____
_____

Reference Check
Candidate Name:_____

Name:_____ Title:_____

Relationship to candidate (former manager, co-worker, etc.)_____

How long have you known him/her?_____

What are the candidate's strengths?_____
_____

What are the candidate's weaknesses?_____
_____

How is the candidate's communication and people skills?_____
_____

How strong are the candidate's management skills?_____
_____

What is the candidate's management style?_____
_____

How qualified do you think the candidate is for this position?____
_____

In your opinion, what qualities make the candidate best suited for this position?
_____

Would you re-hire this person?_____

If not, why?_____
_____

APPLICANT CONTACT SHEET

Date: **Company:**   **Job Opening:**

Applicant	Company	Phone #	Comments

Interview Tracking Form

Applicant Name & Phone Number	Interviewer & Phone Number	1st Intv date	2nd Intv date	Results/ Comments

EMPLOYER-PAID FEE SCHEDULE AND TERMS

The Executive Search Firm of (Recruiter's Company Name) looks forward to providing top quality professionals for your organization.

Services offered through (Recruiter's Company Name) are on an employer-paid-fee basis only.

Fees: The fees for our services is on a contingency basis and are only due and payable if a person is hired as an employee, consultant, or independent contractor, or if any other arrangement is made through our referral. The fee for full-time permanent placements is 25 percent and is based upon the candidate's projected annual gross base salary.

Terms: Total is due upon receipt of invoice.

Guarantee: Should an employee terminate or be terminated for any reason during the first sixty calendar days of employment, (Recruiter's Company Name) will replace the individual at no additional fee. This guarantee is contingent upon payment of our invoice within 15 working days of the employee's start date.

If a candidate is referred to you by (Recruiter's Company Name) and is hired by your organization (including divisions and subsidiaries) within one year of the submittal of said candidate, the placement shall be considered as due to our efforts.

Reference Checking: Before a candidate is hired, we conduct reference checks. In evaluating potential candidates, you, the employer, agree to thoroughly check candidate references independently.

Your acceptance of referrals from (Recruiter's Company Name) constitutes acceptance of this fee schedule.

Recruiter's Name	Client's Name
Title	Title
Company	Company
Address	Address
City, State, Zip Code	City, State, Zip Code

_____   _____
Signature   Signature

_____   _____
Date   Date

Appendix B

RÉSUMÉ AND EMPLOYMENT FORMS:
For Job Seekers

The following forms will keep you as a job seeker organized so that you will be able to track your progress during the job search. The more organized you are, the less likely you will overlook details. Remember not to sit by the phone and wait for it to ring, but to be proactive in your search.

Follow up on all your job leads to put your name back in front of the hiring manager and reinforce your professionalism and determination. In addition, send a thank-you letter to re-sell yourself and your qualifications, as well as to reiterate your interest in the position and the company.

I have included the following forms:

- **CHRONOLOGICAL RÉSUMÉ.** The most widely accepted résumé format, the chronological résumé lists dates of employment, starting from your current employer and working backward. Most employers want to know the number of years you worked at each company.
- **FUNCTIONAL RÉSUMÉ.** This type of résumé focuses on *what* you have done rather than *when* you were employed. This format can help those with gaps in their employment history due to firing, layoffs, prison terms, and parental responsibilities, and can downplay your age if you do not wish to focus on it. You may still be asked to submit a chronological résumé, but the functional résumé will often spark enough interest in you to get you to the next step.

- **ACTION VERBS FOR RÉSUMÉS.** What you say on your résumé is important, but *how* you say it is just as important. Begin phrases on your résumé with action verbs to create action statements such as these: "Developed new policies and procedures manual," "Created successful ad campaign," "Established successful new division," "Increased profits by 25 percent." Use action words that describe your accomplishments, performance on the job, motivation, and passion for excellence.
- **WEEKLY JOB SEARCH GOALS.** This form allows you to see the progress of your job search on a weekly basis. If you write it down, it will not only keep you organized, it will also help you to identify what you are and are not doing that could help you find a job sooner than later. Review the form at the end of each week to identify what you have accomplished and what else you could be doing.
- **NETWORKING ACTIVITY LOG.** Here is another form that will help you set weekly goals for yourself. It is important to document and follow up all your job leads and to track your networking activity. Always ask each contact to suggest another contact.
- **COMPANY/INDUSTRY CONTACTS.** This form is useful for more detailed information about the companies you are applying to, including follow-up information after the interview.

CHRONOLOGICAL RÉSUMÉ

Name
Address, City, State, Zip Code
Phone, E-mail

OBJECTIVE:_____

EDUCATION:

School Name_____ City_____ State_____

Degree Received_____ Major_____ Date of Graduation_____

PROFESSIONAL QUALIFICATIONS:

(In this space, list all the qualifications that are pertinent to the job you are applying for. You may use a paragraph format or a bulleted list.)

PROFESSIONAL EXPERIENCE:

Company Name_____ City_____ State_____

Job Title_____ Dates of Employment _____

(Indicate dates of employment *from* month/year starting *to* month/year ending. Begin with your current employer and work backwards in time.)

Briefly explain: Skills, duties, and accomplishments:_____
_____
_____
_____
_____
_____

(Repeat this information for each position you have held.)

FUNCTIONAL RÉSUMÉ

Name
Address, City, State, Zip Code
Phone, E-mail

OBJECTIVE:_____

EDUCATION:

School Name_____ City_____ State_____

Degree Received_____ Major_____ Date of Graduation_____

SUMMARY OF PROFESSIONAL QUALIFICATIONS:

Briefly explain: Skills, abilities, and accomplishments:_____
_____
_____
_____
_____

(Here is where you emphasize *what* you have accomplished rather than when. You can then list companies you have worked for below.) Example:

PROFESSIONAL WORK EXPERIENCE:

ABC Electronics, San Diego, California
Customer Service Representative

Smith and Jones Associates, San Diego, California
Sales Associate

Johnson Control Systems, Irvine, California
Marketing Representative

ACTION VERBS FOR RÉSUMÉS

Achieved	Created	Formulated	Recruited
Administered	Decided	Founded	Rectified
Affected	Defined	Generated	Researched
Analyzed	Delegated	Governed	Reviewed
Applied	Designed	Grouped	Revised
Appraised	Detailed	Guided	Scheduled
Approved	Developed	Handled	Searched
Arranged	Directed	Illustrated	Secured
Assessed	Distributed	Implemented	Selected
Attained	Earned	Improved	Simplified
Awarded	Effected	Increased	Sold
Built	Encouraged	Influenced	Solved
Calculated	Enforced	Initiated	Stimulated
Catalogued	Enlarged	Inspired	Structured
Clarified	Equipped	Installed	Succeeded
Coached	Established	Instituted	Summarized
Compared	Estimated	Integrated	Supported
Composed	Evaluated	Interviewed	Tailored
Conceived	Examined	Introduced	Taught
Conducted	Excelled	Invented	Transformed
Constructed	Executed	Investigated	Translated
Contracted	Expanded	Launched	United
Controlled	Experimented	Maintained	Validated
Convinced	Facilitated	Mastered	Verified
Correlated	Formed	Recorded	

WEEKLY JOB SEARCH GOALS

Week of: _____

ACTIVITY	GOAL
Review Internet job search tools	_____
Post résumé on Internet sites	_____
Research employer Internet sites	_____
Research companies at library	_____
Review local newspapers	_____
Review trade/business journals	_____
Cold call (on phone/in person)	_____
Apply directly to employer	_____
Complete/update résumé	_____
Send cover letters and résumés	_____
Attend job and career fairs	_____
New networking contacts	_____
Attend industry association meeting	_____
Contact business colleagues	_____
Contact friends/relatives	_____
Make follow-up phone calls	_____
Follow up on job leads	_____
Write thank-you/follow-up letters	_____

NETWORKING ACTIVITY LOG

Date:_____

Contact Name: _____

Company Name:_____

Address:_____

_____

Phone Number:_____ Fax Number:_____

E-mail Address:_____

Action Plan:_____

_____

_____

_____

Appointment Date/Time:_____

Summary of Conversation:_____

_____

_____

_____

Follow-up Plan:_____

_____

_____

Additional Contacts Received:_____

_____

_____

COMPANY/INDUSTRY CONTACTS

Company name: _____

Contact person: _____

Address: _____

Phone number: _____ Fax number: _____

E-mail address: _____

Position applying for: _____

How did I find out about this job? _____

Did I mail, fax, or e-mail résumé? _____ Date: _____

Follow-up date: _____

Results of follow-up: _____

_____

First interview date: _____

Names and titles of people I met with: _____

_____

Second interview date: _____

Names and titles of people I met with: _____

_____

_____

Results and other comments: _____

_____

About the Author

Suzanne L. Rey has been an executive search, human resource and training & development consultant for more than twenty years. Her company, the Rey Edwards Group Inc., has consulted for the real estate development, home building, information technology, and manufacturing industries since 1982.

Suzanne encourages you to contact her with your experiences in the workplace.

She can be reached at:
E-mail: reyedwardsgroup.com
Web site: www.SecretsfromaBodyBroker.com

978-0-595-85276-5
0-595-85276-9

Printed in the United States
69980LV00004B/1-240